CLIMBER'S FIRST AID
WHAT TO DO WHILE
WAITING FOR HELP

Mark S. Fleming

Certified Wilderness Emergency Medical Technician
Certified Emergency Medical Technician (Arizona)

RHACHE

P U B L I S H E R S, L T D.
Preservers of Civilization's Noblest Thing—The Written Word

9 ORCHARD DRIVE • GARDINER• NY •12525–5710
(914) 883–5884• (914) 883– 7169

Climber's First Aid: What to do While Waiting for Help
    by Mark S. Fleming
Front Cover Design and Art by Scott Erik Fleming. Copyright © 1995 Rhache
    Publishers, Ltd.
Illustrations by Carolyn Hutchings Edlund. Copyright © 1995 Rhache
    Publishers, Ltd.
Book Design by Rhache Publishers, Ltd.

Copyright © 1995 Rhache Publishers, Ltd. All rights reserved.

Published in the United States of America
Printed in the United States of America by Tri State Litho, 1 Field Court, Kingston, NY 12401.
0 9 8 7 6 5 4 3 2 1

Rhache Publishers, Ltd.
9 Orchard Drive
Gardiner, NY 12525–5710
(914) 883-5884

Because this book's purpose is to provide information on emergency first aid,
numerous products are mentioned by their trade names. In most instances, these
designations are claimed as trademarks by their respective manufacturers. It is neither
the Publisher's nor the Author's intent to use any of these names generically, but as
examples of the class of products to which they belong.

ISBN 1-887288-00-7

Library of Congress Catalog Card Number: 95–69782

DISCLAIMER

The treatments presented in this book are intended to be practiced by trained individuals. Simply reading this book will prepare you to treat many of the medical issues you may face in the wilderness, but *is not* a substitute for expert instruction in wilderness medicine. Some treatments are abbreviated as the book assumes the closeness of professional assistance. These abbreviated treatments are so indicated in the text. Various topics are not presented, such as instruction in cardiopulmonary resuscitation (CPR) and spinal immobilization, as they are beyond the scope of this book. However, they should be learned completely and competently before venturing out into the wilderness setting.

Specific products identified by their trademarked names are used in the text for purposes of identification and illustration only. Specific brands are not being recommended. Use of any medication or item must be done with caution, subject to the manufacturer's labeling and precautionary statements. No medication should be used unless approved by your physician.

The author and publisher assume no liability for treatments incorrectly executed by untrained individuals or attempted using this book or for use of any medication or device.

To the safety of climbers
throughout the world.

Danger and delight grow on one stalk.
—English proverb

ACKNOWLEDGMENTS

To my mom,
Kay Ellen,
who always encouraged me to try new things,
to live life to the fullest, and, as a great nurse,
fostered my interest in medicine.

To my brother,
Scott,
whose zest for adventure
provided one of the stories in this book,
and who also serves as a reality check for all my ideas.

To my friend,
Casey,
my climbing mentor in Yosemite.
All those early mornings after the late nights
in the Yosemite Lodge Kitchen were worth it.

To everyone I have ever climbed with,
taught climbing to, read about, or watched climb.
You are all a constant reminder of why I enjoy climbing so much.

To those who have contributed the most
to my wilderness medicine education:
Dr. Peter Goth, Dr. Howard Donner, Carl Gilmore,
John Jacobs, Greg Lelo, and Brian Peters, R.N.

Most of all, to
Michelle,
my partner in many respects.
Thanks for understanding about the late nights,
the mess of books around the house, my affair with my computer, and the
reams of paper I asked you to read through and edit for me. I appreciate
your candor, honesty, and unconditional support.

ABOUT THE AUTHOR

Mark Sean Fleming is a State of Arizona Certified Emergency Technician. Additionally, Mark is certified by Wilderness Medical Associates as a Wilderness Emergency Medical Technician and has served as a Wildland Firefighter and EMT. Mark also provides medical support for the Adventure Therapy program at an inpatient treatment center.

Additionally, Mark is the author of wilderness medicine articles found in various magazines including *Climbing, Rock & Ice,* and *Onsight!*

An Arizona-based climber, he has been climbing for more than 5 years and has taught climbing.

FOREWORD

Today, with more and more people leaving the concrete and steel environment in which they live, in search of solitude, beauty, and the quiet openness of nature, not to mention that unclimbed face for which we all search to claim the right to name the route, the number of climbers entering the wilderness has increased dramatically. As a result, some of these climbers are finding themselves, or others, in need of first aid.

Traditional wilderness first aid books have provided in-depth coverage of medical issues in the field, but have often strayed into complex explanations of anatomy and physiology that are useless as blood gushes from an injured leg. Other books have provided a "cook-book" approach to treatment, ignoring even a basic explanation of the systems involved in the various types of injuries. In this book, Mark Fleming has achieved a happy medium.

In *Climber's First Aid*, Mark takes you through a systematic, step-by-step approach to patient care in the wilderness setting. Clear and concise, Mark presents potentially complex medical information in an easy to read manner, allowing those with little or no medical training to become comfortable in administering first aid should the need arise.

Climber's First Aid is very well organized and to the point. From the patient assessment, bone and soft tissue injuries, and environmental hazards, through major system problems, Mark makes it possible to quickly assess most medical situations, allowing you to identify and treat presenting problems. In addition, Mark has provided "Quick Care" sections that provide you an easy reference in assessment and treatment during times of medical emergencies.

Keeping the climber in mind, *Climber's First Aid* is printed on waterproof, tear-resistant paper that withstood a 12-hour submergence test I gave it without signs of smearing or paper damage. Throw the book off El Cap, leave it in the snow, throw it in a river—whatever you do to it, this book will last for many climbing seasons. In addition, the book comes equipped with a binding that can be replaced at any print shop should it suffer damage. *Climber's First Aid* is indeed a valuable, and nearly indestructible, addition to every climber's pack. I will always carry a copy of this book on all my climbing adventures.

Having known Mark for several years, both personally and professionally, I highly recommend this book. Mark's dedication to the sport of climbing and to medicine are of the highest standards, where safety always comes first. I commend Mark for the effort it took to put this book together, the time away from his job, family, and school to bring safety to climbing, and to help move care of the injured to a higher level. This book will help anyone from the novice to the nurse, paramedic, or doctor, and should be part of everyone's first aid kit when traveling into the wilderness—regardless of the type of trip. *Climber's First Aid* is an invaluable asset to your wilderness gear.

Brian Peters
RN, WEMT
3 April 1995
Tucson, AZ

TABLE OF CONTENTS

INTRODUCTION

This book is not like a lot of the other emergency wilderness first aid books. In it you will not find lengthy discourse on the anatomy and physiology of the human body. You will not find technical treatments for situations you are unlikely to encounter while climbing at your favorite crag. And this book doesn't melt during the first rain of the season.

What you will find is a practical approach to emergency wilderness first aid. Technical explanations are limited to what you need to know to deal with the problems you may face. Based on the assumption that professional help is relatively close by, this book takes you step-by-step through the procedures necessary to *stabilize* your patient until help arrives.

Additionally, this book is printed on tear/water resistant paper that can withstand a hurricane. Sure it costs more than others, but 10 years from now you will still be able to use it.

Every effort has been made to present the material in a logical, ordered fashion. Each chapter begins with a true story of a climbing accident, taken from the pages of *Accidents in North American Mountaineering,* or through my personal climbing experiences. Chapters end with a **Quick Care** section, where helpful assessment and treatment hints are given. The book ends with a glossary to help further your understanding of terms, and an outline of what you should take in your first aid kit (and you definitely *need* one).

As with many types of medicine, emergency wilderness first aid is not an exact science. Not every patient will present with the exact same signs and symptoms, and treatments will differ depending on what gear you have at your disposal, amount of time until help can be obtained, and a host of other variables. To become truly proficient at the administration of emergency wilderness first aid, it is advisable to take a Wilderness First Aid or Wilderness First Responder course. Additionally, *everyone* should be comfortable in the performance of cardiopulmonary resuscitation (CPR). Classes can be arranged through your local Red Cross or American Heart Association agencies.

It's worth repeating that this book focuses on the stabilization of injuries. For some situations you will be able to evacuate the patient yourself; for more serious conditions, professional help should be obtained. For those who are traveling to remote regions, books such as *Medicine for Mountaineering* and *The Outward Bound Wilderness First-Aid Handbook* contain excellent information on expanded medical practices.

This book is best utilized by reading it completely, practicing any techniques that you can, and rereading it at intervals to keep yourself prepared in the event of an emergency. Should you ever have to use the treatments described here, and I hope you never do, it pays to be prepared.

Happy climbing!!

Mark S. Fleming
March 25, 1995
Tucson, AZ

1
PATIENT SURVEY

*Injuries can occur as easily on top-rope as on lead, as one climber discovered on **Ultimate Bushwack** (5.5) at Grand Ledge in Oak Park, Michigan. A member of a group of beginners, the climber had unknowingly clipped her carabineer into the belt loop of her jean shorts. When she started to lower off the climb, her belt loop ripped, and she fell some 30–35 feet to the ground. Fortunately, a group of EMT's were teaching a climbing class nearby, and they rushed to her aid. A visual inspection revealed she had sustained multiple fractures, cuts, and bruises. After stabilizing her, they performed a patient survey that greatly aided the emergency personnel who responded. Later communication with the patient revealed that she had suffered multiple injuries including a shattered ankle (requiring surgery), a broken tailbone, and a broken pelvis. By performing a proper patient survey, the responders realized the need for immobilization, thus preventing the possibility of further life-threatening injury.*

A climbing day may be ruined in an instant. Your leader can fall, a top rope climb can turn to mishap if the anchors give way, or a belayer can lose concentration. A typical, everyday rappel can turn into a grisly nightmare for a variety of reasons. Fun turns to disaster in the sweep of a moment.

Most accidents look worse than they really are. Yet, there will be times when injuries are serious. Bones may be broken, a spinal injury might be suspected, or the patient may go into shock. Whatever the emergency, you, as the uninjured (or less seriously injured) person need to assess the situation competently. Not only will this help you in determining the proper course of action, but the information you gather will be of tremendous help to rescuers.

The steps in performing a patient survey are simple. The procedure is methodical, concentrating first on the functions essential for life—respiration and circulation—and then on an assessment of the body as a whole. Using a head-to-toe survey of the patient, important information is gathered towards understanding the complete medical situation. It is important that all climbers, from the "weekend warriors" to the "big wall rats," be familiar with the patient survey. The information gained in these steps may save a life.

Before beginning the patient survey, be sure to put on a pair of latex gloves. This simple precaution may save you from contracting diseases such as AIDS and Hepatitis through contact with blood.

PRIMARY PATIENT SURVEY

ASSESS SCENE SAFETY

Never attempt a rescue or patient survey until you have checked the accident site for additional hazards. Lives have been lost by potential rescuers jumping into action before a dangerous situation was properly assessed.

Look around you. If the accident was caused by rockfall, are there more coming down? Is the area around the patient safe? Is the individual on a cliff, hanging from a rope, or on a small belay ledge? How will you get to him? Can you be safe in getting to him? If you place yourself in a dangerous situation, you might end up giving the rescue squad two victims instead of one. Always ensure any scene is safe for both you and the victim.

Once the scene has been determined to be as safe as possible, an initial assessment of the patient may begin. This includes checking the ABCD's, locating any life-threatening bleeding, and stabilizing the cervical spine.

THE ABCD'S

The ABCD's consist of *A*irway, *B*reathing, *C*irculation, and *D*isability. Checked in this order, the rescuer can be assured that the individual is not in an immediate life-threatening situation from compromised ABCD's. (See illustration on next page.)

AIRWAY

Open the airway by using the chin-lift head-tilt method, or the jaw thrust, and visually inspect the airway for any obstructions caused by the tongue, broken teeth, dirt, or any foreign material. Remove any obstructions with the sweep of a single finger, taking care to not push the obstruction further into the airway. For an unconscious victim, the jaw thrust method is preferred to minimize movement of the spine.

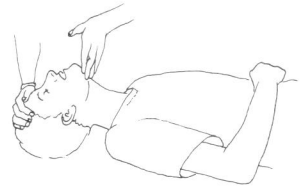

CHIN LIFT

FIRST, establish some responsiveness by shaking the patient and shouting.

A Establish an AIRWAY for breathing. Use the *Chin Lift* method (illustrated on page 2) to tilt the head. Use the *Jaw Thrust* (illustrated on page 4) method if you suspect a spinal injury.

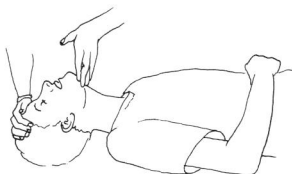

B BREATHING: Look, Listen, and Feel for signs of breathing such as chest movement or air movement from the mouth

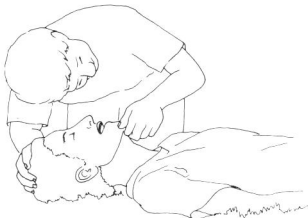

C CIRCULATION: Check for a carotid pulse (illustrated on page 9).

PRIMARY SURVEY

If you can hear, see, or feel air moving through the airway, it is clear. If the patient is making sounds, this indicates that air is moving through the windpipe and that the airway is at least partially open.

Additional indications of an obstructed airway include labored breathing, use of upper chest and neck muscles to breath, and cyanosis (bluish tinge) to the skin. Attempt to clear any airway obstructions before moving on to assessment of breathing.

JAW THRUST

BREATHING

Look, listen, and feel for breath sounds. Look at the chest to see if it is moving. Listen for any breathing or lung sounds. Feel for breath on your cheek.

CIRCULATION

Check for a pulse. Place the tips of your fingers over the carotid artery in the neck and wait for at least 10 seconds. A pulse might be hard to find if it is weak to begin with, if the patient is in shock, or if there is an excessive amount of wind. Clothing also makes it hard to find a pulse.

If there is no pulse and no breathing, begin CPR immediately. If there is no breathing but there is a pulse, begin rescue breathing. If the patient is making any sounds, such as groaning or moaning, a pulse and breathing are certain and no action need be taken.

Both CPR and rescue breathing are covered in CPR classes, and their description is beyond the scope of this book. A review of CPR techniques for trained individuals is included in Chapter 3, and should not substitute for professional instruction.

CHECK FOR LIFE-THREATENING BLEEDING. Look at and feel the patients clothing for moist areas that might indicate the presence of blood. Feel under areas that you cannot see. Should you find obvious life-threatening bleeding, direct pressure and elevation are often enough to stop the flow of blood. Chapter 6 on Soft Tissue Injuries deals with controlling bleeding in more detail.

Do not use this time to deal with minor areas of bleeding. This will be done during the Secondary Survey. Only treat bleeding that is severe and life threatening.

DISABILITY

Injuries to the spinal column can have devastating, and permanent, results. Management of spine injuries should be considered part of basic life support, and will be done during the Primary survey.

Avoid movement of the spine that involves flexion—movement of the chin towards the chest. Other moderate movements are generally safe, and may have to be made to maintain the ABC's.

The initial assessment of the spine should occur during the scene survey. Are there any mechanisms that suggest the possibility of a spinal injury, such as a fall from a cliff, over a waterfall, or a tumble down a scree slope? If a positive mechanism exists, assume the spine has been injured and stabilize immediately. A gentle and steady "in-line" position protects the airway and the spinal cord.

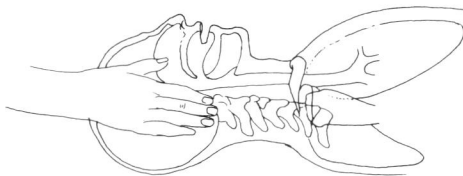

"IN-LINE" POSITION

TREAT THE PATIENT FOR SHOCK

Always assume that the patient has or will go into shock. Maintain an open airway, keep the patient warm and dry, and elevate his legs. Treatment of shock is covered more extensively in Chapter 2.

SECONDARY SURVEY

The secondary survey, illustrated on the next page, is a complete head-to-toe examination of the individual, and should be started only after a complete primary survey has been done. Make sure the patient is comfortable, and talk to him during the whole examination. This lessens his fear, and helps him become part of the examination process. A talking patient can direct your attention to any trouble spots, and keeps you alert to their level of consciousness (LOC). Always ask how what you are doing feels. Given the intimate nature of the exam, examinations should be performed by the same sex, if possible. Always explain what you are doing and why.

As during the primary survey, always look, listen, feel, and smell. Look for bleeding, wounds, unusual shapes or movements, deformities, penetrations, vomit, and excretions. Listen for abnormal sounds, such as crepitus in the bones or sounds from the airway. Feel for wounds, rigidity, hardness, softness, tenderness, or deformity. Finally, note any unusual odors such as alcohol, fruity smells (may indicate diabetes), or bowel odors.

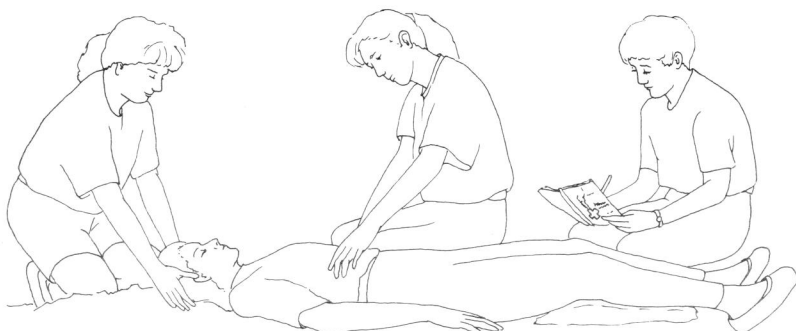

Inspect thoroughly including underneath clothing

| Maintain ABC's & Monitor Vital Signs | Look, Listen, Feel, Smell | Record *ALL* observations in writing |

SECONDARY SURVEY

HEAD

Check the head and face for deformities. Run your fingers along the scalp, checking for blood or wounds. Look in the eyes, noting any pupil abnormalities such as uneven pupils, or excessively dilated or constricted pupils. Ask the patient if he has any vision problems.

Check the ears and nose for fluid and the mouth for any injuries that might impair breathing.

Check the cheekbones for facial symmetry. Do not impede the flow of any fluid from the ears or nose; this fluid might contain cerebrospinal fluid, and preventing its flow can cause pressure buildup in the head which may become a serious problem later.

NECK

Check to see if the windpipe is in the center of the neck. Feel the entire cervical spine in the neck for swelling, deformity, muscle rigidity, or tenderness. See if the jugular veins are distended (bulging).

SHOULDERS

Check the collarbone and shoulders for deformity, tenderness, or pain.

ARMS

Feel each arm from armpit to the tips of the fingers. Check for equal pulse in both arms. Ask the patient to move his fingers, and test for responsiveness by lightly tickling or pinching the palms. If no injury is apparent, ask the individual to demonstrate full range of motion.

CHEST

Push in from the top and both sides with the palms of your hands, noting any instability, deformity, tenderness, swelling, or pain.

ABDOMEN

With the tips of your fingers, check the abdomen for rigidity or tenderness. Break the abdomen into four quadrants, and check each separately. Look for distention, discoloration, and bruising.

BACK

Attempt to check each vertebra along the back. Feel the spine, but minimize movement to the patient. Slide your hands as far under the back as possible. Check for swelling, tenderness, and rigidity.

PELVIS

Press on the front and in from the sides with the palms of your hands. Check for deformity, instability, and pain.

LEGS AND FEET

Investigate the legs from the groin to the tips of the toes. Check pulse in each foot for symmetry of strength. Check sensation and motor skills the same as in the arms.

The secondary survey also includes a look at the patients vital signs and medical history. Again, this is a methodical search that should be accomplished in the order that it is outlined here. Results should be recorded on a sheet of paper every 15 minutes, and given to hospital or rescue personnel.

VITAL SIGNS

Vital signs include level of consciousness, pulse, respiration, pupils, skin signs, and capillary refill. Body temperature and blood pressure are also important vital signs, but unlikely to be obtainable in a wilderness context.

| HEAD-TO-TOE EXAMINATION | VITAL SIGNS |

Head

Neck

Shoulders

Arms

Chest

Abdomen

Back

Pelvis

Legs

Feet

Level of Consciousness

Pupils

Pulse

Skin Signs

Body Temperature

Respirations

Capillary Refill Time

Response to Stimulus (Unconscious Patient)

VITAL SIGNS

LEVEL OF CONSCIOUSNESS

Your level of consciousness reflects brain function. Consciousness can be affected by head trauma, lack of oxygen, low blood sugar, alcohol and diseases of the brain, to name a few.

In the field, level of consciousness is assessed using the AVPU (**A**lert, **V**erbal, **P**ain, **U**nresponsive) method.

ALERT

The person is awake, knows who he is and where he is, and is cognizant of the time and date.

VERBAL

Not fully awake, the patient can respond to verbal commands by opening eyes, moving, or waking up. Being alert to verbal commands indicates a slightly higher level of brain function than when responding to painful stimuli alone.

PAIN

The individual is not awake, does not respond to verbal stimuli, but responds to painful stimuli by opening eyes, moving, or groaning. To stimulate pain, rub the sternum or pinch the muscles at the back of the shoulders.

UNRESPONSIVE

This is a patient who does not respond to any of the above stimuli and is completely unconscious.

Any patient that has lost consciousness for any period of time should be assumed to have a head injury until it can be determined otherwise.

PULSE

Every time your heart beats, a wave of pressure is generated and dispersed throughout the body. These pressure waves can be felt when the tips of your fingers are placed at sites where the major arteries lie close to the skin—pressure points.

For a normal adult at rest, the heart beats between 60 and 90 beats per minute. An athlete may have a resting pulse around 50 beats per minute. Shock, exercise, fear, altitude, illness, and stress can all cause a persons' pulse rate to rise.

There are three areas on the body where the pulse can easily be felt. The first is in the neck, where the carotid artery lies close to the

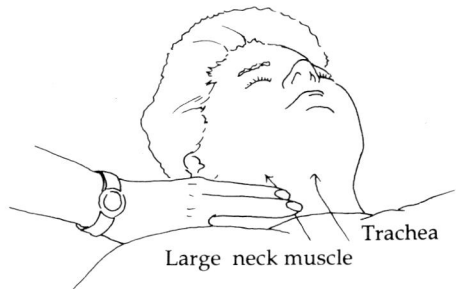

Trachea

Large neck muscle

CAROTID PULSE

skin. Take the tips of your fingers, place them in the grove that is formed on either side of the windpipe, and count the number of beats for 15 seconds. Take this number and multiply it by 4 to get the number of beats per minute.

The second area is at the radial artery in the arm. There is a grove found on the thumb side of the wrist, and the pulse can be counted here.

The third place for locating a pulse is on the top of the foot. Here, the pedal pulse can be found. Mark the spot once you find it since the location is somewhat difficult to obtain.

When measuring an individuals' pulse, note both the number of beats per minute and the strength of the pulse. If it is weak or erratic, make a note. A normal pulse should be strong with equal intervals between beats.

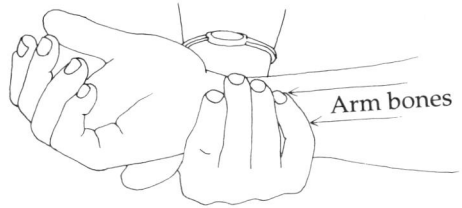

Arm bones

RADIAL PULSE

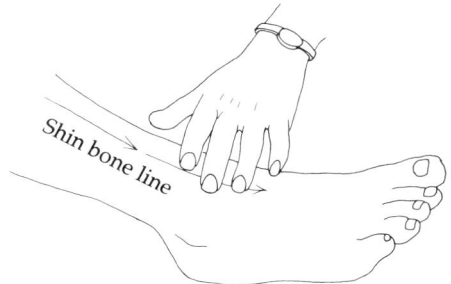

Shin bone line

PEDAL PULSE
After finding the pedal pulse, mark it so that it is easily found again.

RESPIRATION

Count respiratory rates in the same manner you count the pulse. Since it is often hard to hear the patient breathing, especially if there is a wind or a lot of other noise, observe the rise and fall of the chest and count respirations this way. Normal respiratory rate for a healthy adult is 12–20 breaths per minute.

Note the effort and depth of the patients respiration. Deep, unlabored breathing is the sign of a healthy individual. Shallow, labored breathing can indicate a chest injury or some other obstruction that is preventing a full breath from being taken. Irregular respirations may indicate brain injury, and noisy respirations indicate a possible airway obstruction.

If the individuals' breath smells fruity or like acetone, the person may be in a diabetic coma. Breath that smells foul and fecal often indicates a bowel obstruction.

When reporting respiration, include rate, rhythm, effort, depth, noises, and odors. Note respirations every time you check for a pulse.

SKIN SIGNS

The appearance of the skin is a good indicator of the condition of the cardiovascular system. Skin signs include color, temperature, and moisture.

Normal skin is pink in color. In darker skinned individuals, this can be assessed by looking at the nail beds, palms of the hands, soles of the feet, and the lips.

When skin becomes flushed with blood, the skin turns red. This may occur in the presence of heat stroke, carbon monoxide poisoning, allergic reactions, or fever.

When blood withdraws from near the surface of the skin, the skin becomes pale in color. Shock, fright, fainting, or cooling of the skin can lead to this condition.

Cyanotic, or blue-tinged skin, occurs when circulation to the skin is reduced (as in hypothermia) or the amount of oxygen in the blood falls. Cyanosis is indicative of inadequate respiration.

In a healthy person, the skin is warm and relatively dry. As the body temperature rises, skin temperature also rises in an attempt to dissipate some of this excess heat. Hot, dry skin is a sign of fever and heat stroke. Hot, sweaty skin occurs when the body attempts to eliminate excess heat and can also be an indicator of heat illnesses.

When the body needs to conserve heat, as in the case of hypothermia, blood flow is constricted and the temperature of the skin begins to fall. Cold, moist (clammy) skin is an indicator of extreme stress and a sign of shock.

CAPILLARY REFILL TIME

One way to assess circulation is to measure the amount of time it takes the body to refill blood in the areas of the forehead and nail beds.

Press the patients forehead or nail beds firmly with a finger and release. If the white skin at the test site becomes pink within 2 seconds, circulation is not impaired. Should capillary refill be delayed, circulation may be impaired and should be noted.

MEDICAL HISTORY

Obtaining the patient's medical history is useful for several reasons. First, if you did not witness the accident, obtaining a medical history may provide significant insight into any problems. Second, unknown medical conditions may be the cause of, or be compounded by, the trauma. Finally, obtaining a medical history helps you gain rapport with the patient and makes treating injuries easier.

The medical history consists of three components: Chief Complaint

(PQRST), AMPLE History, and *AEIOU*TIPS (the vowels AEIOU and TIPS).

CHIEF COMPLAINT (PQRST)

Ask about the patients chief complaint—what caused him to obtain help. Pain is a common complaint, as is nausea and dizziness. **PQRST** will help you remember the appropriate questions when investigating complaints of pain.

PROVOKES

What provoked the injury? What makes the problem better, what makes it worse?

QUALITY

What adjectives describe the pain? Burning, aching, stabbing, cramping, dull?

RADIATES

Where is the pain? Does it move or radiate? Chest pain from a heart attack often radiates down the left arm and into the neck and jaw.

SEVERITY

How bad, on a scale of 1 to 10 (10 being the worst the patient has ever felt) is the pain?

TIME

How long ago did the pain start? How frequently does it occur? How long does it last?

AMPLE HISTORY

Sometimes accidents can occur for reasons that have nothing to do with climbing, such as allergies, diabetes, or heart attacks. When performing the patient survey, it is important to ask questions that reveal pertinent medical history. Most of these questions will be of importance only to rescuers, but you should ask them anyway. Such questions are called **AMPLE** questions.

ALLERGIES, MEDICATIONS, LAST MEAL

Is the individual allergic to anything? Are they taking any medications? What for? This alerts to possible negative drug interactions. What and when was the last meal they ate (crucial information should they require surgery)? This may also alert you to the possibility of dehydration or a diabetic issue.

EVENTS (RECENT)

Has anything happened recently that might have contributed to the patients condition? Have they been feeling nauseous, dizzy, or anything else? Has this particular event ever happened to them before?

PAST HISTORY

Are there any medical problems you should be aware of? Have they been in the hospital recently? What for? How long? Are they currently under the care of a physician? Why?

Finally, if you should be completing the patient survey on a person who is unconscious, remember to investigate **AEIOUTIPS** (the vowels AEIOU plus the word TIPS). These are possible reasons why a person might be unconscious. Since you cannot ask the patient directly, ask bystanders for this information.

AEIOUTIPS stands for: **A**lcohol, **E**pilepsy, **I**nsulin (Diabetes), **O**verdose, **U**nderdose, **T**rauma, **I**nfection, **P**sychological or **P**oison, **S**troke.

QUICK CARE

PRIMARY PATIENT SURVEY
- ☐ Assess The Scene For Safety
- ☐ ABCD's
  1. **Airway**—Open and Maintain
  2. **Breathing**—Look, Listen, and Feel. Rescue Breathing if necessary.
  3. **Circulation**—If none, begin CPR.
  4. **Disability**—Cervical spine precautions.
- ☐ Check for Bleeding
- ☐ Treat For Shock

SECONDARY SURVEY
- ☐ Look, Listen, Feel, and Smell

○ Head	○ Neck	○ Shoulders
○ Arms	○ Chest	○ Abdomen
○ Back	○ Pelvis	○ Legs and Feet

- ☐ Vital Signs
  1. Level of Consciousness on AVPU scale
  2. Pulse
  3. Respiration
  4. Skin Signs
  5. Capillary Refill Time
- ☐ Chief Complaint (PQRST)

○ Provokes	○ Quality	○ Radiates
○ Severity	○ Time	

- ☐ AMPLE History

○ Allergies	○ Medications	○ Previous history
○ Last meal	○ Events	

- ☐ AEIOUTIPS

○ Alcohol	○ Trauma	○ Epilepsy
○ Infection	○ Insulin	○ Psychological
○ Overdose	○ Poison	○ Underdose
○ Stroke		

2
SHOCK

*The **Flake Pitch** (5.7) on the Guide's Wall at Grand Teton National Park was the scene of an accident in the summer of 1992. Having just clipped into a fixed piton, the leader bent down to remove two pieces of protection he had previously set. This action weighted the piton, causing it to pop out, sending the climber 40–50 feet below to the ledge at the base of the pitch. Sustaining multiple injuries, his belayer stabilized the situation and went for help. Five hours later, after a dramatic helicopter rescue by park employees, the climber was on his way to the Shock Trauma Unit of LDS Hospital in Salt Lake City.*

The term "shock" is often misused when relating the details of a medical emergency. It never fails someone will say, "Did she go into shock?", even when speaking only of a sprained ankle. In the above story, however, the chances of the victim experiencing some level of true shock is almost guaranteed.

Shock involves much more than just having been in an accident. Aside from true cases of shock, where blood fails to become oxygenated, accident victims can also suffer from Autonomic Stress Response (ASR), which mimics true shock in its victims.

Understanding the dynamics of both shock and ASR are important in learning how to treat them in a wilderness setting.

THE SHOCKING TRUTH

Shock is a disorder of the circulatory system. In a normal, healthy state, the body pumps blood efficiently throughout the body, supplying tissues and organs with oxygen and important nutrients. More importantly, our circulatory system provides our brain with the blood and oxygen that it needs to keep us alive and climbing.

Sometimes the body fails to adequately supply (perfuse) our tissues with oxygenated blood. This generally occurs for one of three reasons:

1. Failure of the pumping mechanism (the heart).
2. Problems with the vessels (the container).
3. Low fluid level in the body (blood, water).

There are four types of shock that might occur in a climbing setting—hypovolemic, cardiogenic, vascular, and anaphylactic.

HYPOVOLEMIC (VOLUME) SHOCK

Hypovolemic shock stems from low fluid volume in the body. This can result from a large loss of blood, which may occur in traumatic injuries, or a large loss of body fluids through such means as perspiration, vomiting, burns, or diarrhea.

CARDIOGENIC SHOCK

As the name implies, cardiogenic shock is related to problems with the pumping mechanism. Heart attacks, lightning injuries, and trauma can all cause a critical loss of perfusion even though there is no loss of volume.

VASCULAR (NEUROGENIC) SHOCK

The human body has an intricate system of internal communication, the center of which is the nervous system. The brain is connected to this system and through it tells us when to breath, how much to breath, when to beat the heart, how much blood to pump, and how wide the blood vessels should be that carry the blood. When this system of communication is disrupted, as often happens in isolated spinal trauma, control is lost over the blood vessels. The blood vessels open up in diameter (vasodilation), which decreases the total pressure of the circulatory system. This drop in perfusion pressure results in vascular shock.

ANAPHYLACTIC SHOCK

While truly a subset of vascular shock, anaphylactic shock is so common that it should be discussed alone.

People can be allergic to any number of things. Some to foods, some to microscopic organisms, and some to winged insects, mainly bees. Being stung by bees can cause some people to go into a state of vascular shock as a result of the allergic reaction. In this case, the histamine that the body releases in an attempt to fight the allergen causes vasodilation and results in anaphylactic shock.

AUTONOMIC STRESS RESPONSE

Sometimes, an individual appears to be in shock simply because they are in a stressful situation and their body responds in ways that mirror shock. This is called Autonomic Stress Response (ASR).

Following sudden stress or injury, the body can respond in several ways including fainting, confusion and disorientation, pain-masking, anxiety reaction, and a "shaken" or "dazed" demeanor. These reactions to instances of sudden stress all involve the autonomic nervous system and thus may appear similar to shock or the compensation mechanisms of shock.

It is important to remember, however, that ASR can, and often does, occur *with* true shock. The only difference is that ASR resolves itself, where shock does not. ASR comes in two basic forms.

SYMPATHETIC ASR

This is understood as the "fight or flight" response. If you've ever been in a situation that has scared you greatly, like your first major lead or your first fall, you probably experienced what you called an "adrenalin rush." Adrenalin is a hormone released by the nervous system that speeds up pulse and respiratory rates, dilates the pupils, and generally gets the body ready to fight or take flight. It also stimulates the release of hormones that act in ways to mask pain.

While helpful in allowing people to survive what otherwise might be a deadly situation, the effects of sympathetic ASR make assessment of injuries difficult immediately following an accident.

PARASYMPATHETIC ASR

If you have ever felt faint, or have actually fainted, you have experienced the effects of parasympathetic ASR. Should the pulse rate slow significantly enough to limit perfusion of the blood in the body, especially to the brain, nausea and fainting may be experienced. Again, in a wilderness setting, ASR often complicates the full assessment of any injuries that may have been sustained.

COMPENSATION MECHANISMS

There is a common goal shared between the circulatory system and the nervous system—to maintain appropriate perfusion to specific body parts as needed under various conditions. Additionally, major organs, such as the heart and brain, must be adequately perfused at all times. The body attempts to keep other areas fully perfused as well, such as the outer reaches of the body (the shell), by directing perfused blood when and where it is needed.

The brain and other vital organs, however, are first on the list, and the body responds to any sudden loss of volume, such as from bleeding, by instigating emergency efforts to keep these areas perfused. Available volume is diverted from the less important areas in the *shell*, such as the skin and muscles, and into the vital areas of the *core*, such as the brain, heart, lungs, and liver. To that end, pumping of the heart is increased, and urine output decreases.

At this point the body has "compensated" for the sudden loss of volume.

Should this compensation mechanism be overwhelmed, as in the case of severe volume loss (bleeding, dehydration, etc.), perfusion to the vital organs is reduced. The brain is the most sensitive organ to this drop in perfusion, and the functions that are the first to go will be those such as personality, problem solving ability, and the like.

At this stage of shock, the body is receiving minimal perfusion, and serious damage can occur if the situation is not corrected as soon as possible. Real shock is a serious, life-threatening condition, and most field procedures will only have a temporary effect. The definitive treatment is to seek professional medical assistance as soon as possible.

HOW TO DEAL WITH SHOCK

Since treatment of shock in the wilderness is primarily supportive in nature, the best treatment is prevention. Learn to recognize what sort of mechanisms are likely to result in shock, and know the early signs and symptoms of shock. You will be much better off if you can get to the patient before his compensation mechanisms are overwhelmed.

WHAT YOU SEE

The general symptoms of shock are a rapid, weak, and irregular pulse; rapid, shallow breathing; sweating; pallor; anxiety; nausea; vomiting; and sometimes a partial or complete loss of consciousness. As you can see, most of these signs are expected of a person in a stressful situation.

In a person suspected of having a spinal cord injury, their signs may differ in that they have dry, flushed skin, a slow pulse, neurological problems, and sometimes paralysis.

Persons who are suffering from anaphylactic shock will have flushed skin, swelling, sneezing, hives, and nausea in the initial stages. Individuals with more severe anaphylactic shock exhibit airway obstruction, which, if left untreated, results in death.

WHAT YOU DO

Always assume that shock will occur. Begin your treatment by maintaining the ABCD's as outlined in Chapter 1. If the individual is bleeding excessively, steps must be taken immediately to control the bleeding. A 25% loss of blood volume (1.5 liters) can cause moderate shock, and a 30% loss (2 liters) can result in severe shock.

In the event of anaphylactic shock, aggressive airway maintenance must be performed. If the patient does not have her own medication to reverse the reaction, as do people who know they are allergic to bee stings, be prepared for extensive rescue breathing until professional help can be obtained. The best treatment for anaphylaxis is to avoid the allergen in the first place.

If practical, place the patient on their back. Do this only if precautions for cervical spine injury have been taken. Elevate the legs 8–10 inches, as this will enhance the return of blood to the heart and brain.

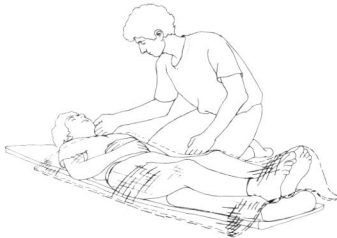

SHOCK TREATMENT
(1) Maintain ABC's and monitor vital signs; (2) Give fluids if appropriate; (3) Maintain temperature within normal limits. Use a covering if needed; (4) Elevate legs 8"–10".

Keep the patient warm. Remove any wet clothing, and protect the patient from the cold ground. Your goal is to maintain the individual's internal body temperature as close to normal as possible. In severe cases of shock, the body loses its ability to produce heat and hypothermia becomes a concern. In this event, external heat must be applied. One way to accomplish this is to place two other climbers in direct contact with the injured person. This is not a direct treatment for shock, but rather an attempt at preventing ancillary problems.

Consider replacing fluids. Do not, however, give fluids if there is a possibility of surgery within the next 6 hours. Fluids in the stomach and anesthetics do not mix. Do not give the person fluids unless they are conscious enough to drink by themselves. Some experts recommend electrolyte drinks, others say plain water is adequate. Try to avoid sugared drinks, since they impede the absorption of fluids in the body, and salty drinks, as they produce nausea.

For patients experiencing cardiogenic shock, having her rest and relax is extremely important. This works to help reduce the load on an already weak circulatory system.

The preferred method of treating shock is immediate evacuation.

Treatment for ASR is supportive in nature. Have the patient lie in a flat position, reassure her that things will be alright, and relieve any pain she might be experiencing. ASR will resolve itself over time.

ANAPHYLACTIC SHOCK

Anaphylaxis is an acute, massive, allergic reaction that involves essentially the whole body. Insect stings are the most common cause of anaphylaxis. In the United States, deaths due to allergic reactions outnumber those by all other venomous animals combined, including poisonous snakes, spiders, and scorpions. Sometimes anaphylaxis is due to drugs, such as penicillin and some serums, and less rarely to foods.

WHAT YOU SEE

Initial symptoms usually appear within 5–15 minutes after exposure; in some cases, they may take up to an hour or as long as 24 hours.

Severe respiratory distress is apparent, appearing and progressing rapidly. Tissues in the upper airway swell causing a lethal respiratory obstruction. Bronchi within the lungs narrow, producing a state akin to asthma but more severe.

The skin is the most common area affected. Hives break out over the body, swelling is obvious around and on the extremities, eyes, and mouth. Eyes can become swollen and red, with conjunctivitis and tearing.

WHAT YOU DO

Most people who go into anaphylactic shock are aware of the conditions that can lead to this problem and carry a kit to help them treat it. This kit generally consists of a syringe and a vial of epinephrine. Let the patient administer it themselves. Once they have recovered, a trip to the hospital for a checkup is essential, as anaphylaxis can return.

If no immediate treatment is available, maintain the ABCD's and evacuate the patient immediately to the hospital. Be prepared to administer rescue breathing, and possible CPR.

QUICK CARE

SHOCK 1. Hypovolemic
2. Cardiogenic
3. Vascular
4. Anaphylactic

☐ Assessment of *General Shock*
   ○ Rapid, weak, irregular pulse ○ Rapid, shallow breathing
   ○ Sweating   ○ Pallor   ○ Anxiety ○ Nausea   ○ Vomiting
   ○ Partial/complete loss of consciousness

☐ Treatment
   ○ Maintain the ABC's   ○ Control bleeding ○ Elevate legs
   ○ Keep patient warm   ○ Replace fluids   ○ Evacuate

☐ Assessment of *Vascular Shock*
   ○ Dry, flushed skin   ○ Slow pulse   ○ Neurological problems

☐ Treatment—Same as for general shock

AUTONOMIC STRESS REACTION

SYMPATHETIC   ☐ Assessment
   ○ Pain masking   ○ Anxiety   ○ "Shaken/Dazed"

☐ Treatment
   ○ Rest ○ Lie Flat   ○ Assurance   ○ Time

PARASYMPATHETIC   ☐ Assessment
   ○ Fainting ○ Confusion/Disorientation

☐ Treatment—Same as sympathetic

ANAPHYLACTIC SHOCK

☐ Assessment
   ○ Initial symptoms develop within 15–20 minutes
   ○ Severe respiratory distress   ○ Hives on skin
   ○ Swelling of extremities, hands, mouth
   ○ Swollen, red eyes   ○ Runny nose

☐ Treatment
   ○ If patient has epinephrine, let them administer it
   ○ Immediate evacuation   ○ Maintain ABC's

3
TRAUMA

Perhaps one of the scariest accidents that can happen while climbing is for a rappel anchor to give way. Such an accident occurred while two climbers were ending their climbing day on **City Girls** *(5.10d) at City of Rocks in Idaho. Having missed the belay anchors as a result of fatigue, the leader had decided to move towards a ledge where he would be able to rest. Once there, he noticed two slings tied around a "pinched" area in the rock. Visual inspection revealed no apparent damage to the slings, and he chose to rappel off them. After testing the anchors with a force he estimated to be equal to that of a rappel, he lowered over the side and suddenly began falling towards the ground. The "pinched" area in the rock had given way, possibly as a result of the preceding season's freeze/thaw cycle. The climber sustained multiple injuries, including lacerations, internal injuries, and a pelvis broken in two places. His right leg and hip joint were impacted 3½ inches into his body, and had to be set with two large fixator pins.*

Severe trauma happens every day in the cities we live in—car accidents, shootings, drowning, head and back injuries, and poisonings to name a few. We usually don't spend much time thinking about them; after all, that is what we pay doctors, paramedics, and EMT's for. It's their job to pick up the pieces and put them back together again.

That won't work, however, if trauma occurs in the wilderness. Doctors and emergency medical personnel are unavailable, and the individual needs immediate attention to save her life. Who is going to help? The answer is you.

From the perspective of a bystander, trauma is ugly and scary. Blood flows freely, the individual is screaming in pain or, worse, is not moving at all, and there are a thousand things to consider. The scene seems totally unmanageable, and the first urge is to run away and pretend it's not even happening.

From the perspective of a rescuer, trauma is ugly and scary. The only difference here is that skills have been learned that can transform this event from a chaotic mess into a manageable situation. Cooler heads prevail, and with the application of skills learned at classes or in this book, a life-threatening situation can be easily and effectively managed by you, the climber in the field.

Every climber should be prepared to deal with some sort of major trauma in her climbing career. Don't think it can happen to you? Take a look through any edition of *Accidents in North American Mountaineering*. The peoples' stories that are in this book are most often those of *experienced* climbers, people who have at one time in their lives probably said "It can never happen to me—*I know what I'm doing.*"

As a climber, there are eight types of trauma that you might come across, either as a direct result of a climbing accident or by virtue of being in the wilderness: cardiac arrest, bleeding, cervical spine injury, head injury, chest injury, anaphylaxis, seizures, and diabetic attacks. You should be able to identify and stabilize each of these until rescue personnel arrive.

CARDIAC ARREST

Cardiac arrest occurs when the heart ceases to beat and blood is no longer being transported throughout the body. Accompanied by respiratory arrest, cardiac arrest is life-threatening and needs to be treated immediately, or the patient will certainly die.

Cardiac arrest can be caused by a variety of events. In the wilderness setting, lightning strike by far outnumbers others as the leading cause of cardiac arrest. Chest trauma and diseases of the heart also contribute to incidence of cardiac arrest.

WHAT YOU SEE

Cardiac arrest is noted by the absence of a heart beat. The patient is unconscious and, depending on the amount of time they have been in cardiac arrest, may have cyanotic skin. Respiration is absent.

Prior to going into full cardiac arrest, the patient may complain of chest pain that radiates down the arm and into the neck and jaw. A "crushing," "squeezing" sensation may be felt in the chest, and the patient may be sweating. No chest trauma is present, and there is no chest wall tenderness.

WHAT YOU DO

Should you reach the patient before they go into cardiac arrest, have the patient rest to reduce cardiac workload, and provide assurance to reduce anxiety. If the pain subsides and the patient stabilizes, transport to a hospital immediately.

Treatment for cardiac arrest requires the immediate initiation of cardio-pulmonary resuscitation (CPR). While a simple procedure in itself, CPR should not be performed by someone who has not been properly trained. The Red Cross and the American Heart Association both offer CPR classes for the general public. If you only take one first aid class in your entire life, CPR is the one. The techniques you learn can save lives. What follows is a refresher for trained rescuers.

CPR must be started immediately, as irreversible brain damage occurs within 4–8 minutes after the cessation of heart function.

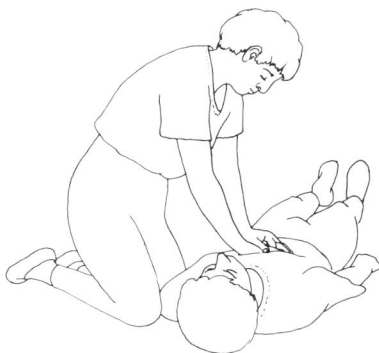

HAND PLACEMENT FOR CPR

Place the patient flat on their back, taking precautions to protect the spine if a spinal injury is suspected. Check the ABCD's to insure that the person is indeed suffering from cardiac arrest. Once this has been confirmed, kneel astride the patient. Place the heel of one hand over the sternum, approximately three fingers above the notch formed where the ribs join the sternum. Place the other hand crosswise over the first and interlock your fingers.

Having placed your hands in the proper location, begin chest compressions. For an adult, depress the sternum about 1½–2.0 inches toward the spine at a rate of approximately 80 times per minute. Avoid rocking your body while completing the compressions, and place your full body weight into each compression.

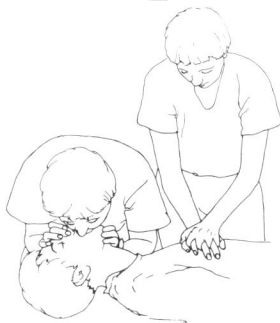

ONE-PERSON CPR

Make 10 cycles of the following: 15 compressions followed by 2 breaths. After these 10 cycles, check again for breathing and a pulse. If none is found, continue CPR. CPR should be carried out until professional help arrives or you are no longer physically able to continue.

It cannot be stressed enough how important it is that every climber learn CPR, and that CPR be performed only by trained individuals. The above description *does not* substitute for qualified instruction.

BLEEDING

Given the extensive network of arteries, veins, vessels, and capillaries in your body, bleeding from injuries often occurs, and generally looks far worse than it really is. Tiny abrasions sometimes bleed profusely, while lacerations may bleed minimally. *Do not overreact to bleeding.* It is important to assess the extent of any bleeding, and treat immediately only those cases that are life-threatening. All other instances of bleeding should be treated during the secondary survey.

Bleeding can occur both outside the body, from open wounds, and inside the body, from closed wounds.

In the case of bleeding outside the body, almost all bleeding can be controlled by direct pressure on the wound. Should this fail, the methods outlined in the chapter on Soft Tissue Injury (Chapter 6) should be followed.

If the injury is internal, bleeding inside the body poses special problems. If the bleeding is inside the head, pressure can build up, causing death or paralysis. Internal bleeding can affect the operation of other organs and should be treated by a physician immediately.

The treatment of severe bleeding takes precedent over the treatment of other injuries except when the patient has no pulse or respiration.

SPINAL INJURY

Every year there are over 10,000 new spinal cord injuries reported. These injuries occur most to people between the ages of 15 and 35.

The spinal cord is the nerve connection between the brain and the rest of the body. In the human body, 33 vertebrae protect the spine from damage. Damage can occur from force that knocks the spine out of alignment, causing injury, or through a direct severing of the spinal cord.

The neck has the smallest vertebrae, allowing for the greatest range of motion. As a result, this area, the cervical spine, is particularly prone to damage. Should the cervical spine be injured, the location of the damage determines if the patient will die, be paralyzed from the neck down (quadriplegia), or be paralyzed from the waist down (paraplegia).

WHAT YOU SEE

Always assume a spinal cord injury on an unconscious accident victim, a person who has fallen from a height, a head injury patient, or someone who has suffered a blow to the head. If a positive mechanism exists, assume the worst.

If an accident victim is alert, well-oriented, has no other injuries, no nausea or vomiting, full range of motion in the extremities with no weakness, and no tenderness or pain in the spine, a cervical spine injury is unlikely.

If you are not sure an individual is free from spinal injury, check for strength and sensation in the toes, fingers, hands, and feet. Ask the patient to push and pull against your hands, and check for bilateral strength in the hands. If the patient complains of paralysis or numbness in any of the extremities, chances are that spinal injury has already occurred.

Check for soft tissue injury over or near the spine, and tenderness or pain in the spinal area.

Should the mechanism of injury indicate that a spinal injury is possible, assume one has occurred and treat the patient accordingly.

WHAT YOU DO

If in doubt, assume a spinal injury until it has been ruled out by rescue personnel.

Your immediate goal should be to stabilize the spine. This can be accomplished in three steps—traction in position (TIP), hand stabilize, and splint stabilize.

The most secure position for transporting an injured spine patient is in the normal anatomical "eyes forward" position. To achieve this, traction the head into position. Grab both sides of the head firmly. While applying gentle traction, move the head until it is in normal anatomical position. Stop the movement if it causes a significant increase in pain, or if resistance to movement is felt.

USING HANDS TO STABILIZE THE HEAD
(Place your forearms on the ground to relieve fatigue and provide stability.)

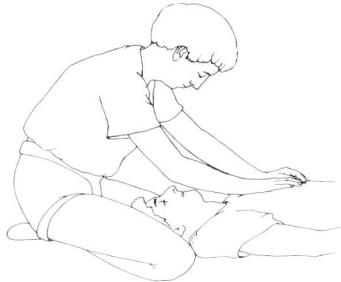

USING STUFF SACKS TO STABILIZE THE HEAD
(Weight with sand or rocks—*never snow.*)

USING KNEES TO STABILIZE THE HEAD
(Helps free hands for other care.)

Once the spine has been tractioned into position, hand stabilize the head. This can be accomplished using the hands, knees, "sandbags," or anything that will prevent the head from moving. At this point, the rescuer at the head is responsible for calling all commands regarding movement of the body. Once at the head, do not leave it until measures to insure continued stabilization have been met.

Finally, splint the spine. This is accomplished using spine boards, litters, and other objects. Immobilization techniques should be practiced prior to their use, and are beyond the scope of this book.

HEAD INJURY

Head injury is the leading cause of death for people in the United States between the ages of 1 and 42. Each year, over 2 million people will suffer head injuries, resulting in 100,000 deaths and 90,000 people suffering some permanent disability.

The primary cause of head injury is from motor vehicle accidents, but outdoor recreational activities, such as climbing, certainly carry the risk of head injury at some point.

Head *injuries* include any injury to the skull and/or brain. These injuries can be open or closed, and may be fatal should they disrupt the heartbeat and breathing. Head injury can also lead to severe physical problems, such as paralysis, as well as a degradation of cognitive functioning. Memory can be affected, and permanent brain damage can occur.

Head *wounds* refer to any injury that occurs to the head that does not involve the brain. A scalp laceration is an example of a head wound.

Regarding the brain, there are three types of injuries to be concerned with. The first, *concussion*, occurs when the brain is jostled as a result of a blow to the head. Individuals often experience temporary brain dysfunction and a loss of consciousness.

Should the brain be forcefully slammed against the inside of the skull, it can be bruised and a *contusion* occurs. If bleeding occurs within the brain, blood pools and a *hematoma* is formed. Since the head is essentially a closed space, this blood builds up inside the head, pinching shut blood vessels, and stopping the flow of oxygen in the brain. If left untreated, the obvious end is death.

WHAT YOU SEE

The signs and symptoms that an individual presents with will vary to a large degree depending on the extent and severity of the injury. Some of these appear immediately, the others develop slowly over time.

CHANGES IN LEVEL OF CONSCIOUSNESS. The patient may only experience unconsciousness for a moment, will move in and out of consciousness, or stay unconscious. Any loss of consciousness is suggestive of a head injury. Conscious patients may appear disoriented, confused, irrational, and incoherent.

VISION DISTURBANCES, HEADACHE, LOSS OF BALANCE, NAUSEA, VOMITING, PARALYSIS, SEIZURES. Any of these may accompany a head injury. Most common are vomiting and nausea. Some brain-injured patients may have seizures.

BLOOD OR CEREBROSPINAL FLUID (CSF) FROM THE EARS, NOSE, OR MOUTH. Some head injuries result in leakage of blood and/or a clear fluid from the ears, nose, and mouth. This indicates that a skull fracture has occurred. The leakage should not be stopped. Doing so may result in a buildup of pressure within the skull (intracranial pressure) that can cause death or permanent injury.

COMBATIVENESS. Episodes of combativeness, aggression, and random strikes at rescue personnel are possible. Should such episodes occur, make efforts to restrain the patient for the safety of the patient and rescuers.

OBVIOUS SKULL FRACTURE, RACCOON SIGN, BATTLE'S SIGN. A quick inspection of the head can reveal the presence of a skull fracture. Two other signs of skull fracture—bruising around the eyes (Raccoon Sign) and behind the ear (Battle's Sign)—generally indicate the presence of a skull fracture.

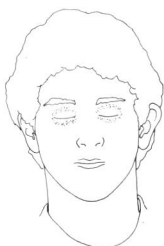

RACCOON'S EYES   BATTLE'S SIGN

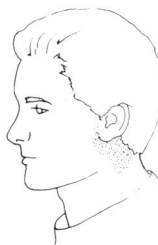

SOFT TISSUE INJURY. If the skin surrounding the skull shows evidence of injury, it is possible that a skull fracture or internal injury has occurred. Look for lacerations, avulsions, abrasions, bruising, and other soft tissue injuries.

SLOW PULSE, IRREGULAR RESPIRATIONS. Serious brain injury is often accompanied by a slow pulse and irregular respirations. Additionally, blood pressure may fall, but this is not easily identifiable in the field.

WHAT YOU DO

Assessment of a brain injury can be difficult. Often, problems arising from medications, use of alcohol, drugs, and traumatic injuries interfere with the recognition of potential brain injuries.

When treating a head injury, begin with the ABCD's. Assume a cervical spine injury has occurred. If the patient is vomiting, place the patient on their side to allow the vomit to drain from the mouth.

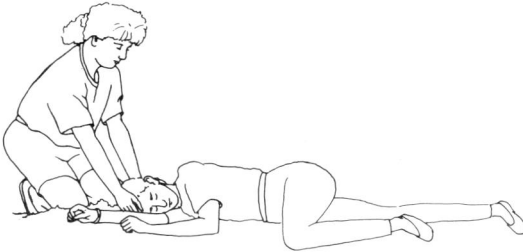

STABILIZING A HEAD-INJURED PATIENT
(1) Roll the patient onto their side. Place their head on their arm with their other arm's elbow and their knees pointed forward; (2)Maintain in-line head position; (3) Take precautions against spinal injury; (4) Monitor their ABC's and Vital Signs; (5) Keep their airway open and clear of vomit; (6) Maintain their body temperature (cover them if necessary).

Control with direct pressure any bleeding from the scalp, but do not prevent bleeding from the nose, mouth, or ears, which might contain CSF (cerebrospinal fluid). Elevate the individual's head, and watch for development of neurological problems, noting them as they occur.

Seek professional help in evacuating the patient as soon as possible.

CHEST INJURY

Of all the traumatic injuries that a climber may sustain while in a climbing situation, chest injuries pose a high rate of occurrence. Many mountaineers have fallen while carrying their ice axes, puncturing chests and piercing lungs as a result. The potential for a rock climber to suffer a chest injury is relatively high, given the nature of some falls on the more extreme sport climbs and the unexpected variances in traditional routes.

Chest injuries can be serious in that they often compromise the respiratory and circulatory systems. The chest contains two of the most important organs in our body, the heart and lungs, and damage to these can be serious.

ANATOMY

The chest cavity consists of the lungs, airway passages, the heart, and the major vessels, the vena cava and the aorta. Protecting these organs are the ribs, 12 in all, the pleura, a sac that surrounds the lungs, and the pericardium, the sac that surrounds the heart.

The boundaries of the chest cavity are formed by the clavicles, rib cage, and diaphragm. All of the ribs are attached to the spine in the back. The upper 7 ribs are attached to the sternum by cartilage, the next 3 are attached by cartilage only, and the final 2 are "floating ribs," attached only to the spine in the back.

Chest injuries include injury to the ribs and the lungs. Some chest injuries will result in damage to the heart, but this is hard to discern in the field and can only be treated at a hospital.

RIB INJURIES

RIB FRACTURES

Ribs can be fractured as the result of a forceful blow, penetration by an object, or blunt trauma to the rib cage.

WHAT YOU SEE

Fractured ribs are evident by deformity and/or discoloration over the injured area. The damaged ribs may feel tender, and the patient may clutch their chest in an attempt to splint the injury. Respiration is often shallow and may be accompanied by sharp, stabbing pains at the injured site.

WHAT YOU DO

A single, nondisplaced rib fracture does not require splinting. Nonnarcotic pain medication may be given.

If the pain is severe, the rib should be splinted. This can be accomplished by taping the site of the injury from sternum to spine with pieces of 1"–2" adhesive tape. Alternatively, wrap an elastic bandage around the entire chest. Do not wrap so tightly that respiration is impaired.

FLAIL CHEST

Should 3 or more adjacent ribs be broken in two or more places each, a condition called flail chest develops. In this case, the rib cage is not a solid unit, and certain sections move independently during respiration. This reduces the pressure formed within the chest cavity, causing difficult and ineffective respiration. Flail chest is generally the result of a massive injury such as a heavy fall against a rock or rockfall onto the chest.

WHAT YOU SEE

Flail chest is indicated by paradoxical chest movement, where sections of the chest move differently with inspiration and exhalation. Additionally, the patient experiences increased respiratory distress.

WHAT YOU DO

Treatment can be accomplished through one of four methods:

FLAIL CHEST
The lung may or may not be punctured.

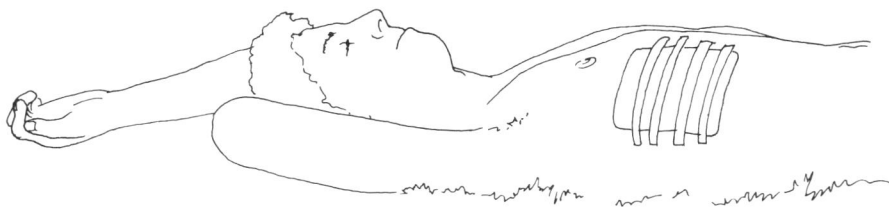

1. Apply pressure to the flailed area with your hand. This is a temporary solution, since the hand will be hard to hold in place during evacuation.
2. Apply a weighted object to the injured area. This can be a bag of sand, a small pack, or sand wrapped in clothing.
3. Position the patient on the injured side with rolled up clothing under the flailed segment.
4. Tape a large pad firmly over the flailed segment.

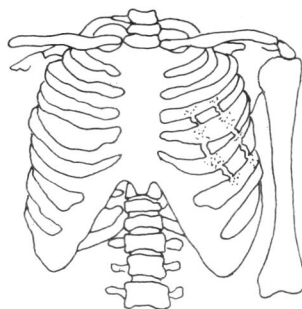

FLAIL CHEST TREATMENT
(1) Place a large pad or sand-filled bag over the flailed area; (2) Tape the pad or bag firmly to the patient extending the tape across the chest *but not* across the back; (3) When transporting the patient, have the patient lie on the flailed side, *not* on the healthy lung side.

Treat the patient for shock, and evacuate immediately.

LUNG INJURIES

Should the ribs be injured, the lungs underneath are often injured as well. As a result, air may be allowed to escape from the pleural sac into the chest, and blood can move from the chest into the lungs. Injuries to the lungs that climbers should be aware of are pneumothorax, hemothorax, tension pneumothorax, open chest wounds, and pulmonary embolisms.

PNEUMOTHORAX/HEMOTHORAX

Should air be allowed to leak into the pleural space surrounding the lungs, a negative pressure is produced that causes the nearest lung to collapse. This can occur as the result of a fractured rib that has lacerated a lung (traumatic pneumothorax), or a weak spot on the lung wall that gives way (spontaneous pneumothorax), or from an open chest injury.

If blood vessels are lacerated as the result of a fractured rib, blood is allowed to move into the pleural space, causing a hemothorax. If more than 1 liter of blood is allowed to collect in this space, the lung is compressed, compromising lung function, and inducing hypovolemic shock.

For reasons that are largely unknown, tall, thin, healthy men between the ages of 20 and 30 are at risk for spontaneous pneumothorax. Eighty percent of these occur while at rest, and can be assessed by a sudden, sharp pain in the chest accompanied by shortness of breath.

TENSION PNEUMOTHORAX

If an injury should break the integrity of the pleural space, a hole that acts as a one-way valve often

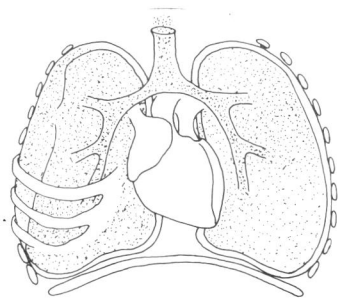

PNEUMOTHORAX

In pnemothorax, air enters the pleural space. However, the lung may or may not fully collapse.

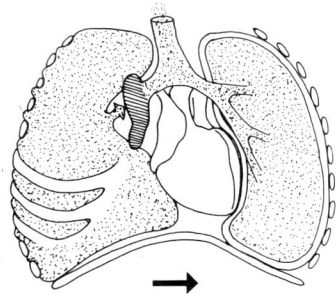

TENSION PNEUMOTHORAX

In tension pnemothorax, air cannot escape, building pressure on the heart and good lung and forcing the trachea to move towards the good lung.

develops. This hole allows air to enter the pleural space, but not escape. As pressure in the pleural space increases, the lung collapses in size. This causes pressure to be shifted to the heart and good lung, and if the pressure gets high enough and exceeds that in the veins, blood cannot return to the heart and death occurs.

WHAT YOU SEE

The patient shows signs of a deviated trachea (windpipe not in center of neck), distended neck veins, bulging of tissue beneath the affected ribs, rapid respiration, weak and rapid pulse, and cyanotic skin. By placing your ear to both sides of the chest, you might be able to hear the differences in respiration. Maintain the ABCD's and evacuate to the hospital immediately.

OPEN CHEST WOUND

Any wound that pierces the pleural space from outside the body and lets in air is considered an open chest wound. If the wound is allowed to remain open, air is taken in and out of the chest, and a sucking chest wound develops.

WHAT YOU DO

By limiting the size of the developing pneumothorax, you increase the ease with which the patient can breath, and the chances they will recover. Seal the hole with some nonporous material. Should the patient experience increasing difficulty in breathing, open the hole to "burp" the wound, and then seal tightly again. This will prevent air that has leaked into the chest from building up. If the patient experiences immediate relief after doing this, the seal may have to be vented at intervals. Listen to the patient to determine the course of action.

Tape

Plastic

Gauze

ASSEMBLING A SEAL

The individual should be evacuated immediately to the hospital.

PULMONARY EMBOLISM

An embolism occurs when clots from veins or globules of fat from broken bones are released and become lodged in the blood vessels of the lungs. This blockage impairs the normal blood flow, and may result in shock.

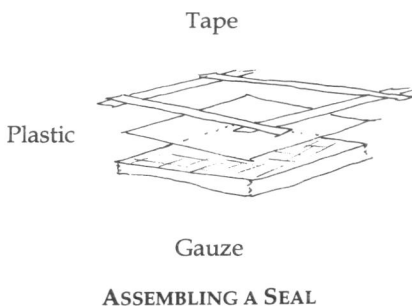

WHAT YOU SEE

The individual feels a sudden shortness of breath, with pain on inspiration, and develops a rapid respiration and pulse rate.

WHAT YOU DO

Treatment requires immediate evacuation and evaluation by a physician.

GENERAL TREATMENT FOR LUNG INJURIES

The following steps should be taken when treating any obvious or suspected lung injury.

1. Open and maintain the airway.
2. Stop bleeding.
3. Quickly seal an open chest wound. Remove or stabilize any impaled objects.
4. Place the patient in the position she is most comfortable in and where she can breath the easiest.
5. Evacuate.

SEIZURES

The brain controls processes in the body through electrical impulses. Sometimes, for unknown reasons, an "electrical storm" occurs in the brain, disrupting communication, leading to muscle contractions, localized motor movement, and sometimes unconsciousness.

Seizures also occur as the result of high fevers, head injury, low blood sugar (diabetes), stroke, poisoning, and epilepsy (the most common).

WHAT YOU SEE

Seizures begin with a short period (usually less than 1 minute) of muscle rigidity, followed by several minutes of muscle contractions. Some people feel the onset of seizures, citing an "aura," while others simply fall to the floor.

The patient may appear cyanotic and may not breath normally. Do not try rescue breathing on the patient during a seizure. Most seizures will resolve themselves before lack of oxygen becomes a problem.

As muscle activity due to the seizure decreases, the patient remains unconscious but the body is relaxed. Pulse and respiration are rapid. Within 10–15 minutes the patient usually becomes conscious, but may remain in a "postictal" state of drowsiness, fatigue, disorientation, and confusion for several minutes or hours.

WHAT YOU DO

Do nothing during the seizure except protect the individual from injury when falling and seizing. The patient will not swallow his or her tongue, and putting anything in the mouth only risks the loss of your fingers.

Once the seizure is over, maintain an open airway, assess for other injuries, provide support to the patient, and evacuate to the hospital. When there, report the onset and extent of the seizure.

DIABETES

Diabetes is a complex disease, afflicting approximately 10 million people. Diabetes is essentially a disturbance of sugar metabolism in the blood, where the body produces too little or too much sugar. Sugar is an essential source of nutrients for the brain, and a balance in the body must be maintained. Some diabetics can experience either hypoglycemia (insulin shock) or hyperglycemia (diabetic coma).

HYPOGLYCEMIA (INSULIN SHOCK)

Hypoglycemia results from the treatment of diabetes, not the disease itself. Hypoglycemia occurs in individuals who have taken too much insulin or fail to ingest enough sugar. Hypoglycemia impairs brain function.

WHAT YOU SEE

Rapid in onset, the person can become irritated, nervous, weak, uncoordinated, and may appear intoxicated. Some people will become unconscious and may have seizures. Pulse is rapid, and the skin is pale, cool, and clammy.

WHAT YOU DO

Administer sugar. If the person is conscious, give her a sugar drink or a candy bar. If unconscious, establish an airway, and place some sugar paste under the tongue. The sugar is absorbed quickly there, and recovery is fast. Once recovered, the patient should see her doctor.

HYPERGLYCEMIA (DIABETIC COMA)

This problem occurs in untreated diabetics and diabetics who have defective or insufficient insulin. Hyperglycemic patients have a high blood sugar level.

WHAT YOU SEE

Hyperglycemia develops slower than hypoglycemia. Patients exhibit a loss of appetite, nausea, vomiting, thirst, and increased urine output. Their breath may have a fruity odor, there may be complaints of abdominal cramps or pain, and signs of dehydration (flushed, dry skin; intense thirst). Unconsciousness is a late sign and a symptom of serious hyperglycemia.

WHAT YOU DO

Treatment is supportive until professional help can be obtained. Maintain an airway and treat for shock. If the individual is alert, give fluids to prevent dehydration.

If ever you are not sure of whether you are dealing with a hypo- or hyperglycemic patient, give some sugar. This action will help the hypoglycemic, and will not affect the hyperglycemic. If the person is conscious, ask when she last ate or when she last took her insulin. Diabetics need to eat at regular intervals, and this may be the problem.

QUICK CARE

CARDIAC ARREST
- ☐ Assessment
  - ○ Absence of Respiration
  - ○ Absence of Pulse
- ☐ Treatment
  - ○ Cardiopulmonary resuscitation (CPR)
  - ○ Immediate professional help

SPINAL INJURY

Assume spinal injury on:
1. Unconscious accident victim
2. Fall from a height
3. Head injury patient
4. Blow to head

- ☐ Assessment
  - ○ Mechanism of injury ○ Weakness in extremities
  - ○ Inability to move extremities
  - ○ Loss of sensation in extremities
  - ○ Tenderness in spine
  - ○ Numbness/Tingling in hands and feet
- ☐ Treatment
  - ○ Traction into position (TIP)
    1. Apply gentle traction to the head
    2. Place head in normal anatomical position ("eyes forward")
  - ○ Hand stabilize the spine
    1. Hold the patients head with hands
    2. Brace head with rocks, pack, clothing, etc.
  - ○ Immobilize the patient
    1. Cervical collar
    2. Spine board (backboard)
    3. Instruct the patient to remain still

HEAD INJURY
- ☐ Assessment
  - ○ Changes in level of consciousness ○ Vision disturbances
  - ○ Headache
  - ○ Loss of balance
  - ○ Nausea
  - ○ Vomiting
  - ○ Paralysis
  - ○ Seizures
  - ○ Blood/CSF from nose, ears, mouth
  - ○ Combativeness
  - ○ Obvious skull fracture
  - ○ Raccoon's Sign
  - ○ Battle's Sign
  - ○ Soft tissue injury on skull
  - ○ Slow pulse
  - ○ Irregular respirations
- ☐ Treatment
  - ○ Maintain ABC's
  - ○ Assume cervical spine injury
  - ○ Place patient on side if vomiting
  - ○ Elevate head
  - ○ Immediate evacuation

CHEST INJURY
RIB FRACTURES
- ☐ Assessment
  - ○ Deformity/discoloration
  - ○ Tenderness
  - ○ Sharp/stabbing pain during inspiration
  - ○ Shallow respirations
- ☐ Treatment—Splint

FLAIL CHEST
- ☐ Assessment
  - ○ Paradoxical chest movement
  - ○ Multiple rib fractures
- ☐ Treatment
  - ○ Apply pressure by hand
  - ○ Apply weighted object
  - ○ Position patient on affected side
  - ○ Tape large pad over flailed segment

LUNG INJURIES

TENSION PNEUMOTHORAX
- ☐ Assessment
  - ○ Deviated trachea   ○ Distended neck veins
  - ○ Rapid respiration   ○ Weak, rapid pulse
  - ○ Cyanotic skin   ○ Differences in lung sounds
- ☐ Treatment
  - ○ Maintain ABC's
  - ○ Treat for shock
  - ○ Immediate evacuation

OPEN CHEST WOUNDS
- ☐ Assessment—Penetration of the chest wall into the pleural space
- ☐ Treatment
  - ○ Limit size of pneumothorax
  - ○ Seal hole with occlusive dressing
  - ○ Burp seal if patient experiences difficulty breathing
  - ○ Immediate evacuation

PULMONARY EMBOLISM
- ☐ Assessment
  - ○ Sudden shortness of breath
  - ○ Pain on inspiration
  - ○ Rapid respiration and pulse
- ☐ Treatment—Immediate evacuation

Seizures
- ☐ Assessment
  - ○ Muscle rigidity   ○ Muscle contractions
  - ○ Rapid pulse and respiration
- ☐ Treatment
  - ○ Protect from harm
  - ○ Maintain open airway after seizure
  - ○ Assess for other injuries
  - ○ Emotional support
  - ○ Hospital visit

Diabetes

Hypoglycemia (Insulin Shock)
- ☐ Assessment
  - ○ Rapid onset   ○ Irritated
  - ○ Nervous   ○ Weak
  - ○ Uncoordinated   ○ Appears intoxicated
  - ○ Rapid pulse   ○ Pale, cool, clammy skin
  - ○ Possible loss of consciousness
  - ○ Possible seizures
- ☐ Treatment
  - ○ Administer sugar either orally or under the tongue
  - ○ Visit doctor

Hyperglycemia (Diabetic Coma)
- ☐ Assessment
  - ○ Slow onset   ○ Loss of appetite
  - ○ Nausea   ○ Vomiting
  - ○ Thirst   ○ Increased urine output
  - ○ Flushed, dry skin   ○ Unconsciousness
  - ○ Fruity odor on breath
- ☐ Treatment
  - ○ Maintain airway   ○ Treat for shock
  - ○ Give fluids if conscious ○ Immediate evacuation

4

FRACTURES AND DISLOCATIONS

Rockfellow Dome at Cochise Stronghold in Arizona was the scene of a bouldering accident in November 1992. Four climbers had been scoping out climbs during the course of the day, and on their return to camp were forced to free climb over several large boulders. Using a granite flake as a foothold, one climber soon found himself falling towards the earth when the flake broke. After falling some 30 feet, inspection of the injured climber revealed a broken pelvis, as well as fractures in both arms. The ulna of the right arm was protruding through the skin, producing an unstable open fracture.

Thank goodness for the human skeletal system. Without the bones beneath our skin, there is absolutely no way we could rock climb. That old advice to "hang on your bones" would be meaningless as we sagged and drooped over the rock. Our skeleton is essential—it keeps us standing upright (essential for walking), holds in and protects our organs, and, most importantly, allows us the necessary rigidity to climb. However, given a strong blow, as in the above story, our bones can crack or break. Sometimes our bones just "pop" out of their sockets, becoming dislocated. While painful, both of these injuries are treatable in the wilderness setting.

ANATOMY

There are 206 bones in the human body. Some bones connect at joints, allowing them to move, such as in the arms and legs. Other bones are fixed, such as in the pelvic region. Joints are held together by ligaments, connective tissue, and muscle. Joint surfaces are covered with cartilage to reduce friction.

The skeleton can be divided into two sections—axial and appendicular. The axial bones consist of the pelvis, spinal column, ribs and skull. The appendicular system consists of the bones of the extremities; the arms and legs.

The scapula (shoulder blade), clavicle (collar bone), humerus (upper arm bone), radius on the thumb side and ulna on little finger side (lower arm bones), and the 22 bones in the wrist and fingers make up the bones of the upper extremity.

The pelvis, femur (upper leg bone), patella (knee cap), tibia and fibula (lower leg bones), and 26 bones in the ankle and foot make up the bones of the lower extremity.

FRACTURES

A fracture is a break in the bone. Fractures can be either open or closed. In an open fracture, there is an open wound over the fracture sight, caused from the inside by the fractured bone itself, or from the outside by the same object that caused the fracture. Closed fractures remain inside the skin, covered by intact muscle. There are several types of fractures, including spiral, crushed, greenstick, and transverse. The specific type of fracture usually cannot be determined without x-ray and will have little effect as to how you will treat them.

CLOSED FRACTURE

OPEN FRACTURE

Beside the obvious problem of a broken bone, fractures can cause complications in other areas. Fractured bones can pinch or sever nerves, causing loss of function and damage to the nerve itself. Fractures can also pinch or sever blood vessels, causing loss of circulation and internal bleeding. Fractures of the large pelvic and femur bones may cause large scale internal bleeding that can lead to shock and death if not treated promptly.

It goes without saying, but should be said anyway, any fracture or dislocation occurring in the wilderness absolutely warrants a visit to the hospital.

WHAT YOU SEE

Fractures are relatively easy to discern. Generally, there will be no doubt as to the existence of a fracture. In a few cases, the physical evidence may not indicate a fracture, but the mechanism of injury will. Whatever the case, following a few steps will help you ascertain if a splint is necessary.

If you suspect a fracture has occurred, the first thing you should do is look. Look at both sides of the body. Does the area in question look the same as the one on the opposite side of the body? Humans are bilaterally symmetrical in nature—we look the same on both sides.

Check the extremity for both bone and joint injury, and circulatory and nerve injury. To assess bone and joint injury, remove any clothing from over the fracture if possible. Look at the injury and attempt to determine if it involves the bone. Feel the limb for tenderness, abnormal bumps, protrusions, or swelling. Look for deformity and discoloration. Listen for crepitus, a grating sound caused by the ends of the bones rubbing together.

To check for circulation, test for the presence of peripheral pulses distal (away from the heart) from the injury. This would be the radial pulse in the wrist and the pedal pulse in the foot. Impaired circulation may also be evident by cold, cyanotic (blue-tinged) extremities. Press on the nail beds and look for capillary refill. A compromise in circulation is most certainly urgent. After 6 to 8 hours, serious damage to the limb may occur if circulation is not restored.

To test nerve function, ask the patient to move fingers or toes. Touch or tickle the extremities and ask the patient if they can feel it.

If, after all this, you are still not sure whether the climber has suffered a fracture, consider the mechanism of injury. Does the accident indicate the likelihood of a fracture? Accidents involving a fall from a height (hard landing after popping off the rock) or a sudden blow to the body (slamming against the rock after flying off an overhanging route) may suggest a fracture. If the mechanism leaves you suspicious, be safe and splint.

WHAT YOU DO

There are a number of steps required in the treatment of fractured extremities. The first is immobilization. Further movement of the injured extremity may cause extensive damage to both circulation and nerves. Immobilization involves the placement of a splint on the injured limb. A splint for a fractured *joint* involves immobilization of the bones above and below the joint. Fracture of a long *bone* requires immobilization of the joints above and below the fracture.

Fractured bones are most stable in their normal "in-line" anatomical position because a fracture disturbs the muscle balance of the limb. When preparing to splint a fracture, it is important to place the extremity in as close to its normal position as possible.

A simple **TIP** will help you appropriately treat a fracture—**T**raction **I**n **P**lace.

First, if possible, remove the clothing in the area of the suspected fracture. Visually inspect the injured area.

Next, check for distal pulses and nerve response. Clean and dress any wounds before applying the splint.

Finally, grasp below the fracture sight and apply a gentle pull (traction) along the long axis of the limb. Support above and below the fracture. Slowly realign the extremity into proper anatomical position. This will help ensure proper circulation in the extremity.

Should you meet physical resistance while trying to realign the extremity, or the patient encounters severe pain, stop the realignment and splint in the deformed position.

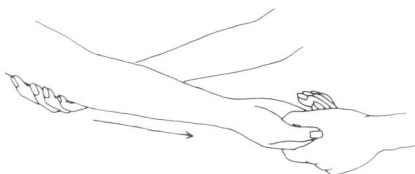

TRACTION AND REALIGNMENT

Should the fracture be an open one, *do not* push the bones back under the skin with your hands. Slight traction should help them go under by themselves, but if they do not, refrain from forcing them under. This will only cause further injury.

Apply a rigid support, generously padded with shirts, pads, etc., to the fracture. This padding will make the patient more comfortable, and will prevent pressure on the limb that may constrict the flow of blood. Secure in place with the use of a cravat, sling, or some strips of cloth or tape.

Remember to remove rings, jewelry, shoes, or anything that may constrict blood flow when the limb begins to swell. Recheck distal pulses frequently. If at all possible, elevate the injury to prevent swelling.

Be creative with material for splinting. Carry a SAM Splint in your pack if possible. This is a semi-rigid splint that can be purchased at any outdoor store. Should one not be available, use a flat tree branch, a piece of the frame of your pack, or whatever you can find. Splinting a fractured leg to the other leg works well, as does splinting a finger to other fingers.

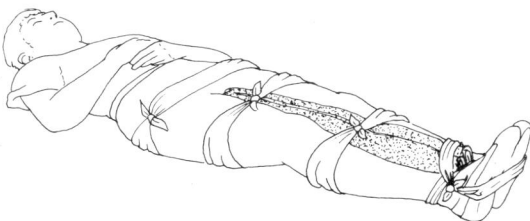

SPLINTING FRACTURED TO UNINJURED LEG

Some fractures involve specific techniques for splinting.

HAND

The hand and fingers should be splinted in the position they are naturally in at rest—the position akin to holding a glass or ball. Fractures to the fingers alone do not require splinting of the wrist. However, for safety sake, if you are not entirely sure the fracture is limited to the fingers, splint the whole hand.

Step 1 (Note hand position)

Step 2

Step 3

Step 4

4-STEPS TO HAND SPLINTING

WRIST AND FOREARM

Splint injuries here with a SAM Splint or the like applied to the palm and underside of the arm, extending from the elbow to the wrist. Elevate the hand above the level of the heart with a forearm sling to decrease swelling. Since the radius and ulna are connected by a tissue band, injury to the one can often cause injury to the other.

UPPER ARM

The humerus can be splinted using a SAM Splint with a sling and swathe. Wrap the SAM Splint on the inside of the arm, over the elbow, and up the outside of the arm for added stability. Applying a sling and swathe will help prevent shoulder and elbow movement.

SLING
Position the hand at heart level.

SHOULDER

A simple sling and swathe is best for this type of fracture.

One sling is used to support the elbow, forearm, and hand. The other is tied around the body and holds the upper arm against the chest, acting as a splint.

If the shoulder is at an awkward angle and immobile, which might occur in a

SWATHE
Secure the sling across the chest.

dislocation, padding should be used to support the arm away from the body if the shoulder cannot be reduced (as explained later in this chapter).

If no triangular bandages are available, webbing can be used as the swath portion. A makeshift sling can be made by pinning the shirt sleeve to the front of the shirt with a safety pin.

KNEE

To immobilize knee fractures, the entire leg must be splinted. A cylindrical splint applied along the length of the leg is recommended. If splint material is limited, a straight splint applied to the back of the leg will suffice. If possible, splint the leg such that the knee is flexed approximately 15°. With the knee well-splinted, the climber may be able to walk short distances.

LOWER LEG

Fractures of the lower leg should be treated by applying a splint to both the knee and ankle. Splints should be well-padded, and are best constructed using a foamlite pad or similar material.

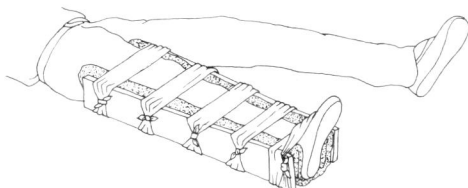

LEG SPLINT

ANKLE

Telling the difference between a fractured ankle and a serious sprain can be difficult. Assume the worst and splint the ankle with a u-shaped SAM Splint that passes around the bottom of the foot and extends up along both sides of the leg. Generously pad.

PELVIS, FEMUR, AND HIP

These are serious injuries, often associated with internal bleeding that, if treatment is delayed, can lead to hypovolemic shock and death. Treating these takes hands-on practice and should be learned in the classroom from a trained professional. They are beyond the scope of this book.

SPINE

The spine is considered a long bone, and any splinting should involve immobilization of the head and pelvis. Spine splinting is a complex skill, and will not be covered in this book.

If you suspect that a climber has suffered a fracture of the spine, take the precautions outlined in Chapter 1. Once this is accomplished, obtain professional assistance in splinting the spine.

DISLOCATIONS

Dislocations occur when a bone is displaced from its normal position in the joint. A dislocated bone may occur by a direct injury, such as falling and landing on your shoulder, or by an indirect injury, such as an arm becoming leveraged in a crack.

WHAT YOU SEE

A shoulder dislocation is apparent as a bump in the area of the joint, with tenderness and pain upon movement and pressure. Dislocated fingers are locked and angulated, or in a "bayonet" deformity. A patella (kneecap) may be found on one side or the other if the knee is dislocated.

All dislocations involve some pain, tenderness, and swelling, and the patient may report a history of dislocations.

APPEARANCE OF A DISLOCATED
SHOULDER

WHAT TO DO

The preferred method of treatment for a shoulder dislocation, if first aid is relatively accessible, is to bind the arm to the chest wall using a swathe or an elastic bandage, and to seek medical assistance. However, if professional help requires hiking on precarious terrain, or is a great distance away, reduction (replacing the head of the upper arm bone in its socket) of the dislocation may be attempted.

If a fracture is suspected along with the dislocation, reduction should not be attempted. *Additionally, reduction should ideally only be attempted by trained personnel as permanent damage can be caused by improper technique!!*

Relaxation of the surrounding muscles is essential. Instruct the individual to relax.

The easiest method requires that you find a flat rock, long log, or similar object that allows the patient to lie in the prone (face down) position with the affected arm hanging freely off. Tie about 15 pounds of weight to the arm at the elbow, padding enough around the elbow to prevent undue pressure on the nerves or blood vessels.

Let the weight hang for approximately 15 minutes. During this time the muscles in the shoulder should fatigue enough to allow

USING WEIGHT TO TREAT A
DISLOCATION

the upper arm bone to slip spontaneously back into the normal position.

An alternate, yet less safe method, requires the use of a level area. Place the patient on his back, sit alongside, and place your stockinged foot on the chest wall near, but not in, the armpit. With a steady, substantial application of traction, pull the patient's arm along the patient's-arm-rescuer's-leg axis. Keep your arms extended, lean back, and use your body weight to apply the necessary force. After 10–15 minutes, reduction should be spontaneous.

Once reduction has been accomplished, secure the limb and seek medical assistance.

If the patella has been dislocated, push the patella back in position while straightening the leg. Fingers can be reduced by grabbing firmly and pulling back into position.

Reducing a dislocated limb is a risky procedure. Nerve and circulatory damage can occur relatively easy. Reduction in the field should be employed only as a last result.

QUICK CARE

FRACTURES

☐ Assessment
- ○ Is the fracture open/closed?
- ○ Bilateral symmetry
- ○ Tenderness
- ○ Unusual bump
- ○ Swelling
- ○ Slow capillary refill
- ○ Absence of pulse in the extremity
- ○ Decreased nervous function
- ○ Mechanism of injury

☐ Treatment
- ○ For bone, splint the joint above and below
- ○ For joint, splint the bone above and below
- ○ Adequately pad splint
- ○ Remove constrictive jewelry, clothes
- ○ Visit hospital

DISLOCATIONS

☐ Assessment
- ○ Bump in area of joint
- ○ Pain
- ○ Swelling
- ○ Obvious joint displacement

☐ Treatment
- ○ Reduce if possible
- ○ Splint if reduction not possible

5
SPRAINS AND STRAINS

*Hardly a climber can be found who cannot tell a tale of a sprained ankle. Such was the case of a young woman who was climbing **Nutcracker** (5.8) in Yosemite. Leading the sixth pitch, she fell for an unknown reason and came to strike the heels of her feet. The blow caused severe sprains in both ankles, resulting in a park rescue and numerous weeks of recuperation.*

Most climbers have suffered a strain or a sprain. While often painful, most climbers walk it off, continue climbing, and think nothing further of it. The reality of the situation is that a strain or a sprain is a serious injury, requiring immediate attention in some cases. Failure to recognize the differences between the two conditions and provide appropriate treatment can result in permanent damage, possibly to the point of ending one's climbing career.

STRAIN

A strain occurs when muscle fiber is either torn or stretched too far. Strains seem to occur most in the extremities and lower back. A strain is usually the result of extreme exertion with muscles that have not been properly warmed up and stretched. Tearing of the muscle fibers can cause bleeding into surrounding muscle and soft tissues.

WHAT YOU SEE

Most strains occur without any precipitating trauma to the joints themselves, and are usually located in areas without joints, such as a hamstring, calf, biceps, or back. There is rarely any pain when the effected area is touched, and little or no swelling.

WHAT YOU DO

Treatment for a strain involves **RICE**—**R**est, **I**ce, **C**ompression, and **E**levation. **R**est the affected area—either limit use or apply a splint in more extreme cases. Apply **I**ce as tolerated for the first 24 hours; this action constricts blood flow to the area, reducing the amount of swelling. When applying ice, be sure to wrap the ice in a piece of cloth to prevent frostbite that may result from direct skin-ice contact.

Apply Compression in the form of an ACE bandage or the like to help provide stability. Do this only on the hands, feet, ankles, or wrists. Compression in any other area can cause vascular constriction.

Finally, Elevate the limb above the level of the heart. This reduces swelling and bleeding, and promotes drainage by gravity.

Heat may be helpful but should not be applied until at least 3 days after the injury.

SPRAIN

A sprain is a tearing or stretching of the ligaments that attach the different bones together. Most sprains leave the joint relatively stable, but a severe sprain can cause instability similar to a fracture. Tearing of a ligament can cause bleeding into the joint and surrounding soft tissue.

WHAT YOU SEE

General signs of a sprain include swelling, discoloration, pain, instability at the joint area, inability to bear weight, and a decreased range of motion in the affected area.

Most frequently, sprains afflict the ankle. When the foot turns into towards the midline of the body and the ankle rotates outward (or inward), as often happens during approaches to climbing sites. The large number of bones in the foot, and the corresponding amount of connective ligaments, greatly increases the possibility of spraining an ankle.

WHAT YOU DO

Assessing the severity of a sprain is important. Have the person put weight on the affected joint and test for load bearing ability. For a sprained ankle, if the person can walk both backwards and forwards normally, a splint is not necessary. A simple treatment of **RICE** and a few days of rest will be sufficient. It might not hurt to see a doctor to assess the severity of the sprain.

If you are within easy walking distance to help, a simple ankle-wrap will stabilize the sprain. For more arduous terrain, or a longer walk out, basket weave taping will provide enough support until the sprain can be checked by a hospital.

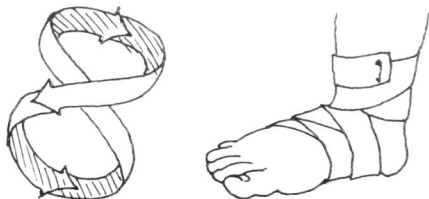

SIMPLE FIGURE-8 WRAP

Should the sprain be more severe—the person cannot put weight on the limb, or the injury suggests the possibility of a fracture—the best course of action is to splint the extremity in the same manner as one would for a fracture, following up with a trip to the hospital.

Determining when it is alright to use the sprained or strained extremity again requires **PFA—Pain Free Activity**. If, after 3 to 4 days, the swelling has resolved and the climber can engage in pain free activity with the extremity, a gradual and restrained return to activity is allowable.

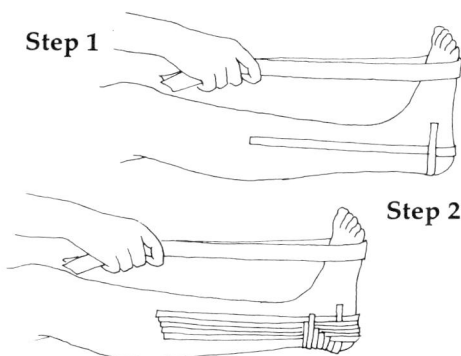

BASKET-WEAVE WRAP
(Repeat Steps Until Wrapped)

TENDINITIS

A tendon is the fibrous cord by which a muscle is attached to bone. Its construction is similar to that of a climbing rope—an outer sheath of tissue covering an inner core of fibers.

Tendinitis is inflammation of a tendon. As the sheath and the tendon become inflamed, the sheath becomes rough. Movement becomes restricted and painful, and the individual feels a grating of the tendon inside the sheath. Fibers can be torn, or irritation from overuse or infection can inflame the sheath causing pain when the tendon moves. There may be little pain when the tendon is at rest.

For climbers, the most often injured tendons are in the arms. Tendinitis develops from overuse, poor technique, and improper warm-up prior to use. Prior tendinitis injuries can also be reaggravated.

Tendinitis can be recognized by redness, warmth, painful movement and sounds of friction or grinding. Swelling may also occur. Treatment for forearm tendinitis includes **RICE** and taping the affected area to reduce movement. A mild analgesic (ibuprofen, acetaminophen) combined with moist heat might relieve some of the pain. Rest is most definitely mandated, as repeated use can aggravate tendinitis, requiring a prolonged absence from climbing.

For extended or more serious cases of tendinitis, a visit to your doctor is suggested.

QUICK CARE

STRAIN
- ☐ Assessment
  - ○ Usually hamstrings, calf, biceps, and back
  - ○ No pain to touch, no swelling
  - ○ General pain on movement
- ☐ Treatment
  - ○ RICE

SPRAIN
- ☐ Assessment
  - ○ Swelling
  - ○ Discoloration
  - ○ Pain
  - ○ Joint instability
  - ○ Decreased range of motion
- ☐ Treatment
  - ○ Assess severity
  - ○ RICE if moderate
  - ○ Splint if severe

RICE
Rest the injured area
Ice as often as possible for the next 24 hours
Compress the area with an elastic bandage
Elevate the area to reduce swelling

6
SOFT TISSUE INJURIES

At Index Town Wall in Washington, a very experienced climber was attempting a routine rappel. It started as a normal rappel, nothing out of the ordinary, but the odds caught up with him. Unaware that his rope was uneven by about 40 feet, the climber rappelled off the end, plummeted to the ground, driving his knees into his face resulting in a split lip. At Whitehorse Mountain, again in Washington, a climber who was leading a pitch accidentally dislodged loose rock, causing it to fall on his belayer. The rock hit the belayer, who was not wearing a helmet, causing a large laceration on the back of his head and a concussion. Numerous other soft tissue injuries have been reported as a result of rock and ice fall, taking a fall while climbing, rappelling off the end of ropes or at too high of speeds (rope burn), and accidents on approach.

It seems virtually impossible to go climbing without sustaining some sort of soft tissue injury. If you live in the Southwest, tissue injuries from sharp shrubs or cactus occur on almost every approach to those remote desert crags. Climbing in the mountains is not much safer either, as tree branches seem to rip and tear at the unwary climber, and the rock itself leaves us battered and bruised with skinned knees and "cherries" everywhere.

For the most part, soft tissue injuries are not very serious. Cleaning the wound, applying antiseptic, and bandaging are all that is required for most minor soft tissue injuries. However, major soft tissue injuries may require immediate and professional care to prevent complications that could inhibit proper healing.

Soft tissue refers to tissue between skin and underlying bone, joints, and organs. It includes fat, muscle, and connective tissue, as well as the small vessels and nerves within these layers.

There are two classifications of soft tissue injuries : Closed and Open.

CLOSED INJURIES

In a closed soft tissue injury, the damaged skin remains unbroken and intact. The most common example is a bruise (contusion), where both tissue and blood vessels beneath the skin are damaged. When blood and plasma begin to leak out of the damaged blood vessels into the surrounding tissues, swelling and discoloration occur.

Hematomas are sometimes associated with closed soft tissue injuries. These occur when blood pools in the tissue surrounding the bruised or damaged area. This often occurs around fractures, when broken bones sever arteries and blood vessels, and in some head injuries. Natural draining of the blood can take from 12 hours to several days, and more serious hematomas may need to be drained by a physician.

Treatment for simple closed soft tissue injuries involves the **RICE** principle : Rest, to allow blood clots to form (both internal and external); Ice for 20 to 40 minutes every 2 to 4 hours; Compression to reduce swelling and bleeding; and Elevation of the injury above heart level to promote drainage by gravity.

When applying ice, be sure to wrap the ice in a piece of cloth to prevent frostbite that may result from direct skin-ice contact.

OPEN INJURIES

In an open soft tissue injury, the integrity of the skin has been compromised. Of primary concern here is contamination of the wound and loss of blood. Open injuries include abrasions, lacerations, puncture wounds, and major traumatic injuries (avulsions and amputations).

ABRASIONS

The most familiar form of abrasion is "road rash" or "rug burns." Climbers most commonly call them "cherries." Abrasions occur when the top layers of the skin have been rubbed off, exposing the tissues underneath. Most abrasions bleed very little, sting painfully, and may be contaminated with debris.

The best treatment for abrasions is to wash out the wound with clean water, apply an antiseptic ointment, such as Neosporin, and a sterile dressing. During the healing process, allow the wound to form a scab by uncovering it from time to time, and keep the area as dry as possible.

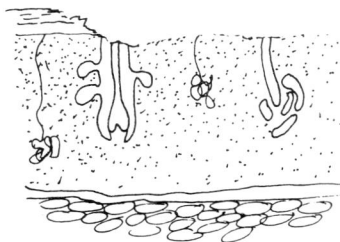

ABRASION

LACERATIONS

Imagine hiking to your favorite crag and being snagged on the leg by the sharp end of a tree branch. You investigate the wound and see a deep, ragged cut, exposing several layers of skin. This is a laceration.

Often lacerations reach deep down into the injured area, severing underlying tissue and ligaments, requiring professional medical care. If the tear in the skin is wide enough, a few stitches may be necessary. Contamination is a significant problem, as dirt often gets deep into the wound and may be difficult, and painful, to completely extract.

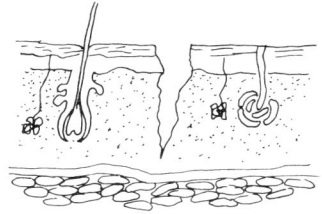

LACERATION

Treatment involves cleaning the wound and applying a sterile bandage to protect the wound from contamination by debris. A butterfly bandage can be used to help keep the sides of the wound together, as well as prevent further contamination. Seek medical assistance. Failure to do so may prevent the wound from healing properly, opening up time and time again, resulting in the formation of a nasty scar.

APPLYING A BUTTERFLY BANDAGE

PUNCTURE WOUNDS

A puncture wound involves penetration of an object into the body. It can be as small as a stick or as large as a tree limb, and as terrifying as an angry landowner's shotgun pellets or a hunter's arrow. Puncture wounds often result in a closed wound. Here, the embedded object serves as a plug in the wound, helping to prevent contamination and control bleeding.

Unless the object has punctured the chest wall or abdomen, removing the object is the first course of treatment. Do so as painlessly as possible, and try to minimize tissue injury in the wound by moving the object as little as possible. If removing the object causes bleeding, try to stop the bleeding as outlined later in this chapter.

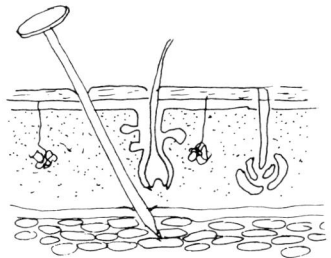

PUNCTURE

If you are unsure about removing the embedded object, and the patients

ABC's will not be compromised by leaving it in, let a doctor do it.

MAJOR TRAUMATIC INJURIES

Major traumatic injuries include avulsions and amputations. Both are caused by trauma to the body.

AVULSION

An avulsion is the tearing-off of a piece of skin. This injury can range in severity from a small flap of skin, such as the fingertip pads that climbers leave on rocks, to a large portion flayed off a limb.

Treatment requires cleaning the avulsed piece of skin and repositioning it over the damaged area. Apply butterfly bandages significantly spaced to allow proper drainage of fluids that may otherwise collect and cause infection.

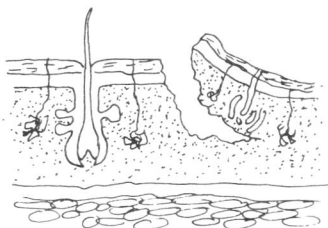

AVULSION

If the avulsed area is greater than 2" in diameter, a skin graft may be required.

Control any bleeding that results form the avulsed wound.

AMPUTATIONS

An amputation is the complete severing of a limb. Amputations may bleed profusely or may not bleed at all, depending on the type of amputation and the condition of the connective vessels and arteries. The most usual type of amputations for climbers involve the fingers or toes.

First, treat the climber for any injuries, such as shock, that may be associated with the trauma that caused the amputation. Control severe bleeding and assess the condition of the patient as a whole.

Next, find the amputated limb. Clean the amputated end of the limb with clean water as best as possible without causing further damage, apply sterile dressings, and place the limb in a plastic bag. Place this bag in ice. This will help preserve the limb for potential reattachment at the hospital.

Do not place the limb directly in ice or cold water. Doing so will cause deterioration of sensitive tissues and render the limb useless at the hospital.

Once stabilized, transport the climber to the hospital immediately.

CONTROLLING BLEEDING

Soft tissue injuries involve some bleeding—anything from a trickle of blood running down your knee from capillary bleeding, to major uncontrollable arterial bleeding from an amputation. It is very important to keep the flow of blood out of the body to a minimum—failure to do so can lead to a decrease in the body's fluid volume and subsequent hypovolemic shock (see Chapter 2).

There are several methods that are effective in controlling and stopping bleeding. The first, and preferred, is direct pressure. Most bleeding can be stopped in a relatively short period of time by taking a sterile bandage and applying pressure directly on the wound. Should the bandages become soaked with blood, replace them with clean, dry bandages. Do not remove the bottom most bandage—any clots that may have formed will be broken loose if you do so.

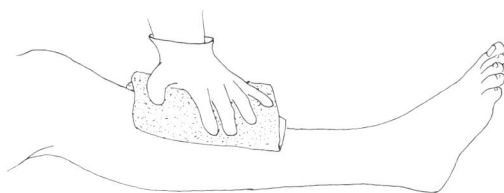

DIRECT PRESSURE METHOD

Before touching any body fluids remember to put on your latex gloves to guard against the transmission of AIDS, Hepatitis, and any other fluid-borne diseases.

When placing direct pressure on the wound, make sure you *see* the wound prior to applying pressure. If you place your hand where you see blood, you may miss the wound entirely. Remove clothing, and clean off any blood that prevents you from visually locating the wound with water.

If direct pressure alone does not stop the bleeding, elevate the limb while continuing to apply pressure. This decreases the amount of blood that is allowed to flow to the limb. This technique is often used in conjunction with direct pressure.

In the Leg   **In the Arm**

If bleeding still persists, apply direct pressure to the pressure points. Pressure points are arteries that lay close to the skin and over bone (see Chapter 3). By pressing on these with your hand, you can stop the flow of blood to the affected limb. In combination with direct pressure on the wound, this should be effective at

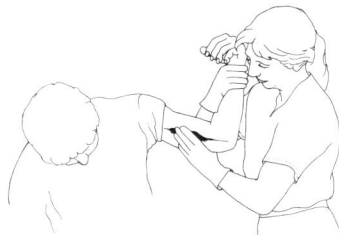

APPLYING DIRECT PRESSURE TO PRESSURE POINTS

significantly slowing or stopping bleeding.

In some circumstances, such as an amputation, bleeding is so profuse from the arteries that a tourniquet is required. **This is a last resort and should not be used unless *absolutely* necessary.** A tourniquet that is left on for an extended period of time can cause tissue damage and, eventually, tissue death. *Tourniquets should only be used when all other measures to control bleeding have failed and the person is in danger of bleeding to death if the flow of blood is not stopped.*

Once you have determined that a tourniquet is necessary, the following steps are critical.

4-STEPS TO APPLYING A TOURNIQUET

STEP 1

First, find a spot close to the injury that is between the injury and the heart. Apply a bandage that is 3–4" wide and several layers thick. Never use a material that can cut the skin, such as rope or wire.

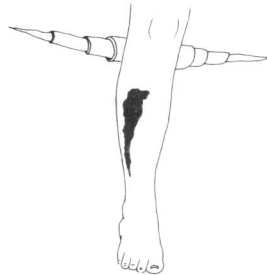

STEP 1

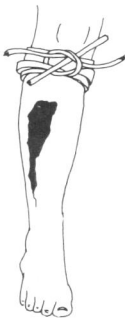

STEP 2

STEP 2

Wrap the bandage several times around the limb and tie an overhand knot. Place a stick on top of the knot, and tie another overhand knot.

STEP 3

Twist the stick until bleeding has stopped and tie the ends of the bandage around the extremity to prevent the tourniquet from unwinding.

STEP 3

STEP 4

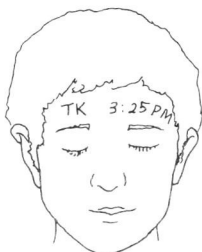

STEP 4

Finally, mark the climbers forehead with the initials "TK" and the time the tourniquet was applied. This critical information informs hospital personnel to the existence of the tourniquet and how long it has been on. Sometimes a tourniquet is missed by hospital personnel until it is too late. **Make sure you mark the climber.** Do not remove the tourniquet once applied; leave this to hospital personnel.

Remember, the decision to apply a tourniquet is essentially a decision to sacrifice the limb to save the life.

CLEANING AND DRESSING

For the purposes of the day climber, cleaning can be restricted to removing large debris by pouring water over the injured sight. Do not dig at the wound to remove debris. Any debris that remains should be removed by hospital personnel.

Once the wound has been cleaned, it is time to dress it. For small wounds, such as abrasions or small cuts, the application of antibiotic prior to dressing will allow the wound to heal faster. For more serious wounds, simply apply a sterile bandage in such a way that circulation will not be compromised in the injured area. Butterfly bandages should not be applied until the edges of the skin have been thoroughly cleaned. Once a bandage has been applied, do not remove it until you are at the hospital.

BLISTERS

Blisters are caused by friction between the skin of the feet or ankles and poorly fitting boots, socks, or foreign bodies within the boot. Sweating enhances blister formation.

Prevention is the key to treatment. At any time during hiking or climbing should you feel a "hot spot" on your foot, immediately stop your activity and remove your shoe. Remove any foreign bodies, straighten your socks, and dry your feet. Apply a patch of Moleskin to the affected area. Be careful not to dislodge the patch when replacing socks and shoes.

If a blister develops, and is small, do not open it. Cut a small hole in a patch of Moleskin and place it over the blister. Minimize walking and allow the blister to heal.

Should a blister develop that is in danger of bursting, drain the fluid yourself. Wash the area with soap and water. Prepare a sterile needle by placing the tip in a flame until red hot. Once cooled, insert the needle into the base of the blister, starting just beyond the blister on the foot. Withdraw the needle and press out the fluid. Do not break the skin. Apply a patch of Moleskin with a hole cut out over the drained blister. Monitor until hike or climb is complete.

If the skin over a blister is already broken, the resulting wound should be cleaned and a sterile dressing applied. Monitor for infection.

Draining

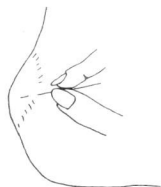

Moleskin Patch

BLISTERS

EYE INJURIES

Rock climbing is dirty business. Wind blows dust and debris, and climbers on the rock above often dislodge rock and dirt that somehow end up in our eyes. Our natural tearing process is often enough to dislodge and wash away the offending object.

When larger objects become lodged in the eye, manual methods must be employed in removing them.

Begin by trying to rinse the object out of the eye. Pour drinking water over the eye from the nose side toward the ear. Do not pour the other way, otherwise you might wash the object into the other eye!

If rinsing fails to remove the object, gently lift the eyelid by the lashes and visually locate the object. With the corner of a sterile gauze pad, lift the object out.

For objects embedded in the eye, stabilize the object by placing a pad over the eye. This will help prevent the patient from trying to use the eye, which will lead to further damage. Evacuate the patient to the hospital.

Grasping the Eyelid

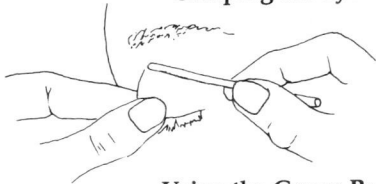

Using the Gauze Pad

REMOVING AN OBJECT FROM THE EYE

QUICK CARE

SOFT TISSUE INJURIES

CLOSED

☐ Assessment
- ○ Bruises
- ○ Tenderness
- ○ Mechanism of Injury

☐ Treatment
- ○ RICE

OPEN

1. Abrasions
2. Lacerations
3. Puncture wounds

☐ Treatment
- ○ Clean wound
- ○ Bandage with sterile dressing
- ○ Remove any embedded objects
- ○ Hospital visit if severe

MAJOR TRAUMATIC INJURIES

☐ Avulsion
- ○ Clean avulsed skin
- ○ Reposition skin over wound
- ○ Apply butterfly bandage

☐ Amputations
- ○ Control bleeding
- ○ Treat for shock
- ○ Find amputated extremity
- ○ Immediate evacuation

CONTROLLING BLEEDING

☐ Direct pressure on wound
☐ Elevate wound
☐ Direct pressure on pressure points
☐ Tourniquet

BLISTERS

☐ Prevention
☐ Moleskin over "hot spots"
☐ Moleskin with hole over small blisters
☐ Drain large blisters, place moleskin as described above
☐ Do not break open blisters
☐ If blister breaks, clean and apply sterile dressing

EYE INJURIES

☐ Natural tearing process
☐ Flush eye with water
☐ Lift eyelid and remove object

7
LIGHTNING INJURIES

In August 1992, climbers and visitors to the Windy Point area on Mt. Lemmon, Arizona were witness to a spectacular, yet brutal, display of natures awesome and unpredictable power. A tourist was watching a climber summit a climb near the overlook. Without warning a bolt of lightning came from the sky and struck the tourist. The lightning jumped from the tourist to the climber, through the metal on his harness, and out his left foot. The tourist went into cardiac arrest. Fortunately, a nurse was nearby and resuscitated him. The climber was thrown several feet along the cliff, suffering damage to his mouth and burns to his feet. Luckily, none of the injuries were fatal. The climbers and the tourists had failed to notice how this sunny summer day had turned dark and overcast in minutes. Recognition of the buildup of a potential lightning storm could have prevented this accident.

The facts are simple. Lightning causes more fatalities in an average year than all other meteorological events combined, including floods, hurricanes, and tornadoes. Lightning causes a serious injury or fatality in about two-thirds of all cases, and permanent injury in about two-thirds of survivors. Lightning is very unpredictable. In Arizona, a thunderstorm can coalesce within 15 minutes, delivering several hundred lightning strikes in a short period of time.

Climbers are at risk of being struck by lightning for two reasons. First, we carry a lot of metal gear. Our figure eight, climbing rack, and metal on our packs are great conductors of electricity. Lightning uses these items to make its travels easier.

Second, climbers play in areas that lightning naturally strikes—ridges, rock spires, exposed cliffs, and areas with large boulders are all potential strike zones. Staying away from these areas during a lightning storm can greatly reduce your chances of being struck.

Lightning is a unique environmental threat in that it can cause multiple injuries of different types, ranging from cardiac arrest to burns and serious fractures. More important, lightning can be fatal.

LIGHTNING DYNAMICS

Lightning is created by a separation of electrical charges, either between clouds, or between clouds and the earth. This separation occurs when strong vertical updrafts drag rain drops through the cloud, resulting in tremendous electrical differences. These updrafts can be caused by convection above hot, flat surfaces—like the southwestern deserts—or by mountain slopes causing horizontally moving air to abruptly begin flowing upwards. The effect is that tall cumulus clouds associated with lightning begin to form.

Normally, air acts as a good insulator, but in the presence of the huge electrical differences associated with lightning, it will break down and conduct electricity. The lightning flash we see is the flow of electrical charges from one object to another (cloud-cloud or cloud-ground) as the objects regain their electrical equilibrium. Lightning is most likely to occur near high and relatively sharp points, like rock spires or ridges. This is because these areas "scrape" the bases of moving air masses, like clouds, and attract the large electrical differences needed for lightning to strike.

There are several types of lightning strikes that the climber should be familiar with.

The first is a direct strike. This is where the lightning strikes a person or object directly and travels through the object on its way to the ground. Lightning looks for the path of least resistance on its way to the ground, and a climber standing on a ridge or rock spire, or loaded with lots of metal gear (an excellent conductor), is the preferred route of travel.

A second type of lightning strike is called splash phenomenon. In this instance, once hit, lightning can "splash" from one person to the next. Splash effects occur when one person is a better conductor than the original object struck and so the lightning arcs to that new conductor.

The final lightning type of concern to climbers is called flashover. Flashover occurs when lightning travels on the outside of the object struck, as opposed to traveling straight through. Clothes drenched in rain or sweat, as often happens during storms and while climbing, helps facilitate this effect. When flashover occurs, moisture in clothing and shoes may be vaporized, blowing these objects off the body and leaving burns on the skin.

Additionally, lighting can also be felt when it flows through the ground after striking the earth. If groups of people are sitting together near the location of a lightning strike, they can all become injured as a result of the flow of electricity.

LIGHTNING INJURIES

The majority of lethal injuries caused by lightning are from cardiopulmonary arrest—the cessation of both breathing and heart functions. However, rapid initiation of CPR can save a climber's life. According to statistics, over 70% of the people who are struck by lightning and suffer cardiopulmonary arrest will live if they are given prompt and correct CPR.

In the event that a climber gets struck by lightning, always check the ABCD's and perform CPR if necessary.

Other injuries may occur directly or indirectly as a result of lightning strike. When struck by lightning, the muscles are forced into violent contractions by the electrical current, often causing fractures (Chapter 4), cervical spine injuries (Chapter 3), and dislocations (Chapter 4). The impact of a lightning bolt can be powerful enough to throw a person several feet into the air, into an object, or off the edge of a cliff.

Additionally, a climber struck by lightning may have these symptoms: disorientation and dizziness, inability to speak, unconsciousness, bleeding (Chapter 6), shock (Chapter 2), and burns.

Lightning burns are distinctive in nature. One type of burn, a linear burn, follows the areas of heavy sweat concentration, traveling down the trunk and then splitting to flow down both legs. Other lightning burns may form feather-like patterns in the skin, while still others may leave pock-mark circles ranging in size from a few millimeters to a centimeter in diameter. Most lightning burns are either first or second degree in nature. A few may be more serious third degree burns.

A first degree burn is one that leaves the first layer of skin red and painful to the touch. An example of this is a mild sunburn. The burn heals in 4 or 5 days accompanied by peeling of the skin. Treatment for this may only require a cool cloth or medicated sunburn spray to help alleviate the pain.

Second degree burns injure both the top and middle layers of the skin. These burns are very painful to the touch. The skin appears red, mottled, wet and blistered, and turns white with the application of pressure. Blisters make take up to 24 hours to form, with complete healing of the burn taking 5 to 25 days if there is no infection.

Treatment involves cleaning the burn with water, preferably sterile water, and covering with a moist, sterile dressing. Do not apply any ointment or creams, as many of these are ineffective and may do more harm than good. In addition, burns of this nature should be inspected by your doctor.

Third degree burns are extremely serious. These burns destroy all layers of the skin, and also involve muscle and other sensitive tissue immediately under the skin. The burnt skin appears leathery and dry, with a gray color to it. Ironically, this most serious burn is not as painful to the touch as most of the nerves and blood vessels in the area have been destroyed. Painful first or second degree burns may surround the sunken area comprising the third degree burn.

Initial treatment of third degree burns is the same as for second degree burns, but immediate evacuation is essential. These types of burns usually require hospitalization and multiple skin grafts to heal.

Finally, a major concern when dealing with a burn victim is dehydration. Burns often result in a large loss of fluid from the body as damaged capillaries fail to prevent massive leaking of blood serum. If the climber is awake and oriented, encourage him to drink as much fluid as possible.

SAFETY FROM LIGHTNING

There are a number of ways to avoid being struck by lightning while climbing.

The first is being aware that a storm involving lightning may be imminent. Check the weather report the day before you leave. If the forecast is for thunderstorms in your climbing area, keep an eye out for developing storms.

If a storm does develop, there is a thumbnail formula to determine how far away it is. After observing a lightning strike, count (one thousand one, one thousand two, . . .) the number of seconds until thunder is heard. Since sound travels approximately 1 mile in 5 seconds, taking the total time counted and dividing it by 5 will give a good approximate distance to the storm. Thus, if the time interval is 15 seconds, the storm is about 3 miles away.

Should you be caught in a lightning storm while bouldering or hiking near a grove of trees, seek an area with the highest density of *low* boulders or trees. To reduce your chances of being hit in a group of tall boulders, stay away from any object that is 5 to 10 times your height, keeping a distance of one-half the height of the object away.

Contrary to popular belief, do not take shelter under the closest tree or rock. While this may protect you from the elements, the lightning may arc into the area or pass through as a ground current if the cave is in a depression or drainage.

Remove any gear you have on that might act as a conductor. If you are in a group, spread out as far as possible so the lightning does not travel from one member to another, either via splashing or through ground currents.

An immediate rappel off an exposed climb is clearly called for. Lightning can travel down cracks in rocks, along newly formed waterfalls, and along your wet rope. It is paramount to your safety to immediately, and safely, get off the climb.

SAFETY WHEN LIGHTNING STRIKES

Frequent lightning strikes (multiple bolts above) are extremely dangerous, while occasional strikes are dangerous. Seeking shelter in a deep cave is safer than being outside, but only if you can avoid touching the walls and being near the cave entrance. Being outdoors is relatively safe if you avoid trees and boulders (see main text) and remove your gear. You should either sit on something that is dry and nonconducting or squat with your feet facing downhill and your hands off the ground. The arrows in the above illustration show the course lightning takes through the ground.

If the storm approaches so fast that an immediate rappel is not possible, tie into a secure anchor and wait the storm out. Since your rope can act like a conductor, lay it across rather than along possible paths of ground current (seams in the rock, cracks, rivulets of water, etc.). To prevent electrical current from flowing through the chest and spinal cord, do not tie into a chest harness.

Should you be fortunate to find a *deep* cave, crawl in as far as possible. Do not touch the walls, and stay away from the entrance since lightning can flash across it and into the cave.

The best place to be is in your car. The metal frame will help disperse the charge. Don't touch any of the metal inside the car, and sit squarely on the seat. Be careful getting there, though. Avoid walking along ridges and other places where lightning is likely to strike.

Finally, if any of the following occurs, know that a lightning strike may be immanent : crackling or buzzing noises (like laundry static or bees buzzing), bluish glow or corona around a person or object, or hair standing on end. Get to safety as quickly as possible.

QUICK CARE

TYPES OF LIGHTNING

Direct
Splash
Flashover
Ground

INJURIES

☐ Types
- ○ Cardiopulmonary Arrest
- ○ Burns
- ○ Fractures
- ○ Bleeding
- ○ Shock
- ○ Unconsciousness

☐ Treatment
- ○ Check ABCD's
- ○ CPR if necessary
- ○ Assessment of other injuries

BURNS

First Degree
☐ Assessment
- ○ Red skin
- ○ Painful to touch

☐ Treatment
- ○ Cool cloth
- ○ Medicated sunburn spray

Second Degree
- [ ] Assessment
  - O Extremely painful
  - O Red, mottled, wet skin
  - O Blisters within 24 hours
  - O Skin blanches white
- [ ] Treatment
  - O Clean with water (sterile)
  - O Apply clean, cool dressing
  - O Hospital

Third Degree
- [ ] Assessment
  - O Leathery, dry, pearl gray skin
  - O Lack of pain
  - O Involvement of muscle and deep tissue
- [ ] Treatment
  - O Clean with water (sterile)
  - O Apply clean, cool dressing
  - O Hospital

SAFETY

Watch for lightning storms
Become the lowest point in the area
Avoid standing near tall trees or rocks
Avoid ridges, hills, summits
Immediate rappel off climb
Crawl in a deep cave if available
Get in car and leave

8
BITES, STINGS, AND LEAFY THINGS

The base of the cliffs at Sleepy Hollow, Mohonk Preserve, Shawangunks, was the site of a battle between man and bee. A climber was approaching the cliffs when he upset a swarm of feeding yellow jackets, who promptly attacked and stung him multiple times. With a history of being allergic to bee stings, a condition that becomes worse with each new attack, the climber went into full anaphylactic shock. Fortunately, the climber recovered fully with no ill effects. This attack, however, compels us to be aware of the potential problems that can occur should bees be encountered while climbing.

The good news is that for most adults, a venomous bite or sting is harmless. Most animals won't give a full injection of their precious venom to something they know they can't kill.

The bad news is that for some the results can be deadly. A bee sting that causes only mild pain to me might send my climbing partner into potentially fatal anaphylactic shock.

When we go climbing, we share the environment with a variety of creatures that can be harmful to us. Of concern to climbers are venomous snakes, bees, arachnids, fire ants, and some plants.

VENOMOUS SNAKES

A venom is a poison that is excreted by animals. This venom is produced with the intent of killing prey for food. However, should a climber provoke a venomous animal enough, natural defense mechanisms take over and the animal may use its precious poison on you.

Worldwide, there are approximately 45,000 reported snake bites a year, about 8,000 of them occurring in the United States. Some 15 people a year die from these bites, and most of these deaths could have been avoided. Humans often try and out maneuver snakes, finding, much to their chagrin, that the snake is extremely fast, and end up getting bit. These bites usually occur on the arms below the elbow and the legs below the knee.

There are two classes of venomous snakes in America: the rattlesnake, copperhead, and cottonmouth, whose venom affects the nervous and circulatory system; and, the coral snake, whose venom affects the nervous system only.

RATTLESNAKES

Rattlesnakes snakes belong in the pit viper class, and have the following characteristics: triangular heads, thick bodies, and pits between the eyes and nostrils. Coloring and length varies with the species, but most have earthy browns, grays or reds. Four feet is the average length with a set of rattlers capping the snake's tail.

RATTLESNAKE

Rattlesnakes usually rattle before they strike, *but not always*. Theory has it that the rattle is a way of warning hoofed animals of their presence.

As a rattlesnake strikes, retracted fangs extend and sink into the skin of the victim. Venom release is regulated by the snake, and can apparently be adjusted for the size of its victim. The age, size, and health both of the snake and the victim affects the venom toxicity, and the victims response to it, respectively. Fang marks do not necessarily indicate envenomation, as 20–30% of all bites do not envenomate.

WHAT YOU SEE

Signs and symptoms of envenomation include swelling, pain and tingling at the bite site, tingling and metallic taste in the mouth, fever, chills, blurred vision, and muscle tremors.

WHAT YOU DO

Treatment should be immediate: gently clean the wound with antiseptic, if possible, and apply a sterile dressing. Remove any rings, watches, etc., that may cause constriction of the limb should it begin to swell. Keep the level of the bite at heart level or below (gravity helps prevent spreading of the venom); keep the patient quite, hydrated, and comfortable. Undue excitement causes the circulatory system to speed up and the venom to spread faster. If practical, immobilize and transport the victim. Rapid evacuation is essential.

If you have a device such as the Extractor by Sawyer Products, use it. Do not cut the skin and apply suction within 3 minutes of the bite. This will not guarantee that all the venom will be removed, but studies indicate up to 30% will be. *This does not substitute for a visit to the hospital.*

Do not cut the bite and suck out the venom—then there are two people who need to go to the hospital. Do not apply tourniquets, pressure bandages, ice, or electric shock. These are all ineffective and ultimately do more damage than good.

COPPERHEAD

The copperhead is identified by a copper-tinged head and buff, pink, or hazel body color. Body markings are described as being hourglass- or dumbbell-shaped. Copperheads are found in the eastern half of the United States, with a range from Massachusetts to Florida, and as far west as Texas. The average copperhead is as long as a 1.5 meters.

Because of their willingness to share close quarters with humans, copperheads are responsible for almost two-thirds of the poisonous envenomation in the United States. Considered to have a mild venom, treatment is the same as for the rattlesnake.

COTTONMOUTHS

A member of the pit viper family like the rattlesnake and copperhead, the cottonmouth, or water moccasin, has a flat, broad head, heavy, thick body, and a darkish color. They inhabit the marshy, swampy environment of the Mississippi Valley, ranging from southern Virginia to Florida, and west to eastern Texas.

Cottonmouths are more aggressive than rattlesnakes, but their venom is considered less toxic. Treatment should, however, be the same as for the rattlesnake.

CORAL SNAKES

"Red and yellow kill a fellow, red and black, venom lack." Coral snakes average 23–32" in length, are thin and brightly colored, and have adjacent red/yellow bands. These snakes are found in the southern and southwestern states, inhabiting dry, open brush ground near water sources. Coral snakes have short fangs which limit their bites to the toes, fingers, and lose folds of skin. Docile in nature, they generally bite only when provoked.

Symptoms from a coral snake bite may not appear until several hours after being bitten. They include drowsiness, weakness, nausea, rapid pulse and respiration progressing to complete respiratory failure as a result of the neurotoxic nature of the venom.

If an individual has been bitten by a coral snake, or a snake you suspect is a coral snake, get them to the hospital immediately. Always assume that a coral snake bite has included envenomation. Monitor the patient's breathing, and perform CPR if needed. Do not delay in getting to the hospital.

BEE STINGS

Like snakes, bees generally use their venom for killing prey. However, curious humans often get too close to bees and sometimes get stung. Bee stings can occur as a single sting or multiple stings. The chances of becoming ill are greatly increased with the number of times the victim has been stung.

WHAT YOU SEE

Stings from bees and wasps usually result in immediate pain, swelling, and redness. The stinger is often left in the victim, so immediately scrape or flick it out with the edge of a credit card or some similar material. Do not pull it out with your fingers as this may squeeze any residual venom into the victim.

WHAT YOU DO

Treatment includes gently cleaning the wound with an antiseptic soap. Ice or a cold cloth may be placed on the wound to help relieve pain and swelling. Discourage the victim from scratching the wound, as this can lead to a secondary infection.

For a small percentage of people, being stung by a bee can place the victim in anaphylactic shock. This is a life-threatening situation, and should be treated as discussed in the chapter on shock (Chapter 2). Most people who know they are allergic to bees carry an epinephrine kit, and it should be administered by them since they have been trained in its use.

BRAZILIAN (AFRICANIZED) HONEY BEES

This type of honey bee was brought to Brazil from Africa in an attempt to make a hybrid that would produce more honey. Somewhere along the genetic hybridization, certain characteristics emerged that are considered to be dangerous. Africanized bees, or "Killer Bees," have a marked increase in their sensitivity to any disturbance in their colony, are able to communicate rapidly between colonies, and, most importantly, are able to respond quickly and aggressively in attacking intruders.

In 1957, the bees swarmed in Brazil and began migrating north to the United States. In 1993, they reached the southern borders of Texas and

Arizona, and attacks by these bees have been recorded. As of yet, no humans have been killed in the United States.

These bees are highly aggressive in their attacks. While they are not any more venomous than other similar bees, the fact that they attack in groups generally leaves the victim with multiple stings. Prevention is the key to avoid being attacked. If you are hiking in the wilderness, wear light-colored clothes that cover your arms and legs. Avoid wearing perfumes and other scents that might alert the bees to your presence. Africanized bees only attack as a means of defense, so if you don't mess with them, they probably won't mess with you.

Should you be attacked by Africanized bees, *run like hell!* Seek shelter in a car or some other area that the bees cannot get into. When running, make efforts to run through bushes and brush areas; hopefully, this will slow down the swarm. Cover your head as much as possible, since the area around the eyes is their preferred area of attack. If you or a member of your party should get stung, observe for and treat any allergic reactions, and evacuate to the hospital.

ARACHNIDS

Arachnids include spiders, scorpions, and tarantulas. Arachnids are mostly terrestrial, are wingless, and have four legs. All are carnivores, living in a variety of habitats around the world.

BLACK WIDOW SPIDER

The black widow spider kills only 4 to 6 people a year. The venomous female is about 4 centimeters long, and is shiny black with a red "hourglass" design on its abdomen. The adult male is not venomous, is smaller in size, and lacks the characteristic hourglass design.

The loosely-constructed webs of the black widow spider are found between rocks, in rodent holes, wood piles, and dark areas of houses. The female often hangs upside down.

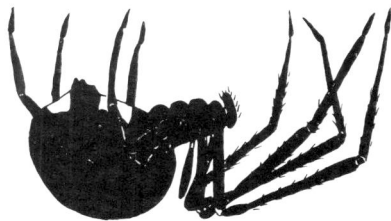

FEMALE BLACK WIDOW SPIDER
Drawing shows the abdomen marking. The black widow's body is approximately the size of a dime.

WHAT YOU SEE

Initially, the bite of the black widow is not painful. Very soon after feeling a small pinprick, if even that, a dull numbing pain develops in the bite area and rapidly spreads to neighboring muscle groups within 15 to 20 minutes. If the bite is on a lower extremity, the abdomen may become rigid. If on an upper extremity, the shoulder, back, and chest are apt to be in pain and experience muscle spasm. Nausea, vomiting, headache, and sweating are likely symptoms of black widow bite. In more severe cases, paralysis, seizures, shock, and respiratory arrest may occur.

WHAT YOU DO

Treatment begins with visually locating the bite. Look for areas of swelling or small bite marks in the skin. Once this has been accomplished, clean the wound thoroughly. Apply an ice pack to both relieve the pain and to slow down the spreading of the venom. If the bite is on an extremity, apply a splint to reduce mobility and the flow of venom. Immediately evacuate the patient to the hospital, bringing the dead spider with you if possible (although this will not be likely in the wilderness). Monitor the climber for serious effects of the bite during transport.

BROWN SPIDER (BROWN RECLUSE)

The brown spider is smaller than the black widow and can be recognized by a violin-shaped mark on its head. Localized populations of recluse spiders have been found in Arizona, Wyoming, California, Florida, New Jersey, North Carolina, Pennsylvania, and Washington, DC. Both sexes are dangerous, and they prefer to hang out in woodpiles and rocks.

The bite of the brown spider is usually painless. Most victims do not notice they have been bitten until several hours later, when the pain begins and the bite area becomes red and swollen. Small blisters may begin to form. Over a period of several days, more local tissue is destroyed by the venom, leaving a dark, ulcerous wound, eventually to be replaced by a scab.

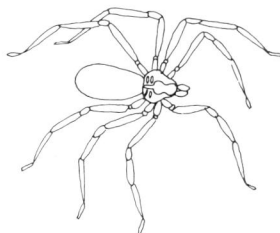

BROWN RECLUSE SPIDER
Drawing shows the violin-shaped marking on the head. The brown recluse's body is smaller than a dime. Unlike the black widow, both male and female brown recluses are venomous.

Reactions like those of the black widow are relatively uncommon, but if they do occur will do so in the first 24 hours.

Treatment includes cleaning the bite thoroughly and applying an ice pack to alleviate the pain. Seek medical attention as soon as possible to prevent further tissue damage.

TARANTULAS

Except for some exotic species located in the tropics, tarantulas are not harmful. As mean as they look, their fangs are too weak to penetrate our skin very deeply, and any bite will only result in a small local wound. The biggest reaction you can expect is some mild swelling around the bite area.

SCORPIONS

Only one type of scorpion in North America is potentially fatal to humans—a small, yellowish species that resides in Mexico, Arizona, and New Mexico, called the Bark Scorpion, or by its generic name *Centruroides*. Fatalities occur mostly in the very young and the very old.

The typical Bark Scorpion is about 2" long, slender, and straw-colored. There is a tiny protrusion at the base of the stinger located on the tail. The sting of the Bark Scorpion has killed more people in Arizona than have the bites of all poisonous snakes combined.

Scorpions like to hide out in woodpiles and under rocks. They also have a propensity for boots, sleeping bags, and clothes. Shake clothing out before putting on. Shake sleeping bags before using.

SCORPION

WHAT YOU SEE

A scorpion sting is indicated by a pricking sensation at the bite area. This is followed by a burning pain, swelling, redness, numbness, and tingling.

WHAT YOU DO

Treatment includes cleaning the wound thoroughly. Apply ice and immobilize the affected area. Transport immediately to the hospital.

In more severe cases, symptoms include impaired speech, tightened jaw, muscle spasms, nausea, vomiting, convulsions, and respiratory and circulatory distress. The initial treatment is the same, but now time is of the essence. Treat any additional problems as they arise.

TICKS

Worldwide, only the mosquito transmits more disease than the tick. Ticks reside in numerous areas of the United States and have different seasons in which they are active. Ask at a local outdoors store for information about your area.

Ticks are considered dangerous because they act as vectors for diseases such as Malaria, Yellow Fever, Tick Fever, Relapsing Fever, Spotted Fever, Tularemia, Babesiosis, and Lyme Disease.

Preventing exposure to ticks is of utmost importance. There are available on the market several types of tick repellents—look for the ones with "permethrin" in them. Visually inspect the body several times a day for ticks, as they will often crawl around for several hours before attaching themselves.

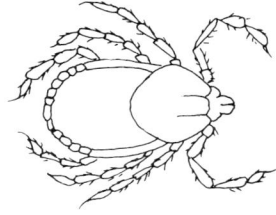

TICK
Ticks are significantly smaller than a dime. They are hard-bodied with 8 legs. When engorged with blood, the body becomes rounded, soft, and rubbery.

Diagnosis of tick-related illnesses in the field is difficult. Any tick bite accompanied by rash, fever, or flu-like symptoms requires medical help.

To remove a tick, grasp it as close to the skin as possible with a pair of tweezers or gloved fingers. Pull the tick straight out, being careful not to squeeze the bodily fluids of the tick into the wound. Clean the wound thoroughly. Do not apply nail polish, alcohol, or burn the attached tick. While these techniques may cause the tick to back out of the skin, the tick will more likely die, preventing easy removal.

It is important that after any activity in an area where ticks are suspected, a thorough "deticking" be conducted. Visually inspect the body, especially the scalp, for ticks. If you have a pet that you took climbing with you, detick it as well.

FIRE ANTS

In 1971, a survey was conducted in Mississippi, Georgia, and Alabama, where there were reported over 12,000 stings by fire ants. Of these, over 6,000 required treatment for secondary infection, 76 had anaphylactic reactions, 8 required skin grafting, and 5 required amputation of a limb. This survey was completed over 15 years ago, and the distribution of the fire ant in the United States has spread.

The fire ant is a small, reddish-brown to black ant that lives in mounds with long radiating tunnels. These nests are made in the ground and surrounded by a mound 18" to 3 feet in diameter, but only an inch or two high. The tunnels may radiate as far as 80 feet from the center of the mound, and lie only about a quarter of an inch or so below the surface.

The usual time for fire ant envenomation is during the summer months, when the ant and victim are most active outdoors. Fire ants are unique in that they do not run—they attack. Within a half-minute hundreds of ants can be crawling on the climber. Not only do they bite, they sting as well.

WHAT YOU SEE

Once the ant has bitten its victim, it begins to spin around the bite area, stinging the climber in a halo-shaped area. Envenomation can be confirmed by the halo pattern of bites, and an intense burning and itching sensation that lasts about an hour. Within a few hours, the bite area begins to turn red and swells.

WHAT YOU DO

Most people have no adverse reactions to the bite of the fire ant, save for a possible skin infection as a result of scratching the wound. However, as in the case of bees, one must be concerned about the possibility of an anaphylactic reaction. Watch a victim of a fire ant bite for any allergic reactions and treat as outlined in Chapter 2 (Shock).

POISONOUS PLANTS

Much of the climbing that is done in the United States is done in wooded areas. Given this fact, the chances that you will come into contact with one of the three main poisonous plants—poison ivy, poison oak, and poison sumac—are high.

These three plants cause rashes in outdoor participants through contact. The stems and leaves of these plants contain an immunogenic resin that can cause allergic reactions on the skin of exposed individuals. So powerful are the chemicals contained within these plants that only one exposure is needed to sensitize an individual, and the next exposure will cause a severe reaction. This sensitization persists for years. In fact, nearly 10% of Forest Service field employees are incapacitated by exposure to these plants each year.

POISON IVY

WHAT YOU SEE

The initial symptoms of exposure are itching, redness, and a burning of the skin. These symptoms may appear within a few hours or may develop within 72 hours. In some cases, lesions may develop where contact with the skin has been made.

WHAT YOU DO

When exposure is first detected, take steps to minimize further exposure. Leave the area, or, if you are certain of the plant's identity, avoid touching further patches of the plant.

Immediately wash the skin with soap and water. This must occur within 30 minutes of the initial exposure as the resins of the plants will bind to the skin after that time. At that point, treatment will consist of washing the affected area with soap, following it with an application of some sort of corticosteroid. Your drugstore or doctor can give you suggestions on which to buy.

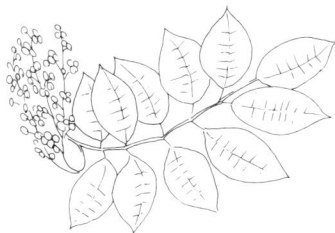

POISON OAK

POISON SUMAC

Avoid touching other areas of the body so as not to spread any resins that may remain. Furthermore, destroy any clothes that are suspected of having come in contact with the offending plant.

If you are treating a climber who has been exposed, wearing latex gloves will reduce the chances that you will become affected as well.

Some people react more violently to these plants than others, in particular children, and in this case, professional medical attention should be sought.

QUICK CARE

VENOMOUS SNAKES

1. Rattlesnakes 2. Copperhead 3. Cottonmouth 4. Coral Snakes

☐ Treatment (*Rattlesnake*)
- ○ Clean bite area ○ Apply sterile dressing
- ○ Remove rings, watches, etc.
- ○ Minimize exertion during transport
- ○ If Sawyer Extractor is available, use within 3 minutes of bite

☐ Treatment (*Coral Snakes*)
- ○ Maintain ABC's ○ Immediate evacuation

BEES

☐ Assessment
- ○ Presence of stinger ○ Swelling ○ Redness

☐ Treatment
- ○ Watch for anaphylaxis ○ Apply ice
- ○ Remove stinger carefully ○ Avoid scratching
- ○ Clean wound ○ Epinephrine if needed

FIRE ANTS

☐ Assessment
- ○ Halo-shaped bite area ○ Redness
- ○ Intense burning and itching ○ Swelling

☐ Treatment
- ○ Clean wound ○ Apply ice ○ Monitor for anaphylaxis

ARACHNIDS

Black Widow Spider

☐ Assessment
- ○ Numbing of bite area
- ○ General muscle numbness in 15–20 minutes
- ○ Nausea ○ Vomiting ○ Headache ○ Sweating

☐ Treatment
- ○ Clean wound ○ Apply ice ○ Splint extremity ○ Monitor ABC's
- ○ Watch for anaphylaxis ○ Immediate evacuation

Brown Recluse Spider
- ☐ Assessment
  - O Redness   O Swelling   O Small blisters   O Ulcerous wound
- ☐ Treatment
  - O Clean wound   O Apply ice   O Seek medical attention

Scorpions
- ☐ Assessment
  - O Prickling sensation at bite   O Burning pain   O Swelling
  - O Redness   O Numbness   O Tingling
- ☐ Treatment
  - O Clean wound   O Immobilize extremity   O Apply ice
  - O Monitor ABC's   O Immediate evacuation

Tick
- ☐ Assessment
  - O Body of tick on skin
- ☐ Treatment
  - O Pull tick straight out   O Clean wound

POISONOUS PLANTS
1. Poison Ivy   2. Poison Oak   3. Poison Sumac
- ☐ Assessment
  - O Itching
  - O Redness
  - O Burning of skin
  - O Possible lesions
- ☐ Treatment
  - O Minimize further exposure
  - O Destroy contaminated clothes
  - O Wash skin with soap and water within 30 minutes
  - O Apply corticosteroid
  - O Wear latex gloves while treating

9
HEAT ILLNESS

When my brother and I first started climbing, we did some climbs at Indian Cove in Joshua Tree. Scott was leading a climb, one of his first, when he yelled down to me that he needed to rest. I asked what was wrong, and he told me he felt nauseous, light-headed, and weak. He managed to make the rest of the climb, although he felt cold and had chills. When he got down, I observed that he was suffering from mild heat exhaustion. This took place in March; it was deathly hot with a burning sun, not the kind of weather you would expect for the beginning of Spring. A combination of exertion and not drinking enough fluids brought on this potentially serious problem. From then on, we always made it a point to keep hydrated.

All machines create heat as they operate. Friction in a car engine causes heat buildup, and the operations of the human body do so as well. Heat buildup can be disastrous; in a car, it will cause the engine to overheat and stop working. In the human body, it can be deadly as vital organs, most importantly the brain, are literally boiled in our own blood. The body has numerous ways to prevent potentially deadly heat from being retained, but should these heat regulating strategies fail, several types of heat illnesses, including heat cramps, heat exhaustion, and heat stroke (hyperthermia), can develop.

HEAT MANAGEMENT

The body has several mechanisms to insure that it dissipates the buildup of potentially lethal heat. The first reaction is to send more blood to areas near the skin; hence, the flushed appearance of people who are hot. Once this is accomplished, the body tries to eliminate heat in one of two ways: by **convection**, in which moving air picks up the heat off the skin and takes it away, or by **radiation**, where heat is simply radiated to the surrounding air without the aid of moving air currents.

Should neither of these methods work, the body begins to sweat. Sweating causes heat loss by the method of **conduction**, or evaporation of sweat. This method, however, has its limitations. A person can sweat several quarts of fluid every hour, but the ability of the body to sweat becomes limited as dehydration sets in and the fluid content of the body is reduced. Sweating also becomes ineffective should the humidity of the air be greater than 60%, preventing evaporation of your sweat into already saturated air. At this point, the body has run out of options for dissipating its stored heat. Consequently, further heat generation will cause the internal temperature of the body to rise, often resulting in fatal consequences.

The types of illnesses caused by heat depend on a number of factors, including body type, level of hydration, climate, and amount of physical exertion. Given the scope of movement and work involved in rock climbing, it is important to be aware of four types of heat illnesses: heat cramps, heat response, heat exhaustion, and heat stroke.

HEAT CRAMPS

Heat cramps are most likely to affect the climber who has had a very strenuous day and has not replenished his or her liquids at regular intervals. When most people climb, they sweat, and as a result they drink. This is good, but it only tackles half of the problem. Heat cramps occur because of a loss of both fluid *and* salt. Water does not contain very much sodium, so, although it does replace the lost fluids in the body, these internal fluids become increasingly dilute. As fluid dilution occurs, the muscles lose important nutrients and begin to cramp.

WHAT YOU SEE

Cramps begin suddenly, starting as a mild tingling sensation but often progressing to severe and incapacitating pain. They usually start in the extremities and the abdomen. The climber may feel faint or nauseated, but generally remains alert. The skin is pale, cool, and moist; a reflection of the heavy sweating the climber has done.

WHAT YOU DO

Treatment for heat cramps is simple—stop climbing and get out of the sun! Move to a shady, cool spot, and if you is feel dizzy or weak, lie down for a moment. When you are strong enough to drink by yourself, water mixed with a package of Gatorade mix (or similar sports drink) should help to replace *both* lost fluids and salt. Do not give take salt tablets since this will make an already nauseated person feel even more so, plus Gatorade (or the equivalent) tastes a lot better.

Do not rub the cramps. Not only is this a useless therapy, it adds to the your discomfort. The cramps should begin to dissipate by themselves within a few minutes of salt and fluid replacement. Further exercise can cause more dehydration and lead to more serious heat injuries. Just take the day off, or be your partners' belay slave, and stock up on fluids. Stretch before you go climbing again, and make sure you are properly hydrated before you begin to climb.

Heat Response

When the mechanisms for dissipating heat are working properly, the core body temperature is still at or near normal. The person (not patient, yet) is responding normally by reducing exercise, removing clothing, replacing fluids, and so on, as needed to maintain an appropriate comfort level.

While at this point no specific treatment is required, heat response is an indicator that the delicate balance within the body has been disturbed. Pay attention to maximizing heat losses and increasing fluid intake and replacement.

Note the color condition of your urine. Urine output is a better indication of hydration level than thirst. Your urine should be light yellow in color and you should feel the need to void at a normal and healthy rate. Should your urine be darker and less frequent than normal, you immediately know to increase your hydration level.

Thirst is a poor indicator of hydration. By the time you feel thirsty, fluid depletion may be at a dangerous level. Drink before you become thirsty, drink often, and drink copiously!!

Heat Exhaustion

Heat exhaustion, sometimes called heat prostration or heat collapse, is caused by a significant loss of body fluids through sweating in people who are working in the intense heat.

What You See

Unlike heat cramps, there are warning signs that heat exhaustion is occurring. The climber may experience headache, weakness, fainting, nausea, and vomiting. The skin is pale, cool, and clammy, and the climber may be disoriented. The patient's pulse and respiration is elevated, and she might complain of being very thirsty. While these symptoms may, and often do, occur gradually, they can occur without warning, resulting in the climber's sudden collapse.

What You Do

Treatment for heat exhaustion is simple—get the climber out of the sun into a shady place and replace lost fluids. Again, that Gatorade package will come in handy. Have the patient lie down, remove any excess or restrictive clothing, and sponge and fan the patient to help lower the body temperature. Sorry to say, but in the event of heat exhaustion, your climbing day is absolutely over. Once the person feels better and thinks they can move on, head to the car and drive to the nearest emergency room. A quick stop there will ensure that the climber is on her way to recovery and that there is no hidden damage.

HEAT STROKE

Simply put, heat stroke can kill—a one-way ticket to that great climbing crag in the sky. When heat stroke occurs, all of the body's temperature regulating mechanisms have failed and the internal temperature can skyrocket to over 105°F. Heat stroke is the second leading cause of death in athletes.

When the body is in a state of fluid depletion, heat exhaustion results in a loss of effective sweating (sweating stops) and precedes a rise in the body's core temperature. Should the body be faced with an extreme heat challenge, such as staying in a sauna too long or hard exercise in a hot environment, a dangerous rise in core temperature can occur before fluid levels are depleted (still sweating).

WHAT YOU SEE

A climber may experience confusion, delirium, and even coma, as the brain is literally boiled by the hot blood surging through it. Conscious patients may act like they are "crazy" or "on drugs." The skin is hot and dry to the touch, although some patients may be sweating profusely. Skin color is pink or ashen, pulse and respiration very rapid. As a rule, suspect heat stroke in any person acting strange in a hot environment. This may be hard given the loony nature of climbers, but do your best.

Many patients will report having spent long periods of time in the sun without replacing fluids.

WHAT YOU DO

When confronted with heat stroke, *time is critical*. Move the patient to a cool and shady area. Remove all their clothing and have the person lie flat and rest. Immediately fan the patient, adding cool water to help bring down the temperature. Apply water to their pressure points, as large blood vessels lay close to the skin in these areas and cooling the blood will help lower the body temperature.

If the person is alert enough to drink water by themselves, give liquids orally. Use that Gatorade package. Do not force liquids on a person who cannot drink by themselves.

Once the person appears to be feeling better, skin color and pulse/ respiration rates have stabilized, and they are alert, get them to an emergency room. This time there is no choice. Without professional attention, they may suffer irreversible damage. Damage to organs from heat stroke may not be evident for days. If you are in a position to send someone for help without moving the patient, do this immediately. Remember, time is of the essence. If in doubt, assume heat stroke.

One warning about cooling a person with suspected heat stroke. As strange as it seems, a person can develop *hypothermia* while they are being cooled for hyperthermia. Keep a lookout for the symptoms of both.

FLUID BALANCE

Maintaining the proper fluid balance in your body is essential. A person can live for weeks without food, but only a few days without water. Fluid balance encompasses an equilibrium between fluid losses (kidneys, respiration, skin, other routes) and fluid intake (directly and through foods). During periods of heavy activity, such as rock climbing, fluid loss often exceeds fluid intake, and the balance is shifted in a dangerous way.

On average, an adult loses 1.5–2.0 liters of water per day. This number increases with exertion, altitude, and physical well being. Climbers at high altitudes can lose 4–5 liters of fluids per day.

The best indicator of fluid loss is volume and color of urine. A 24-hour output of less than 0.5 liters, or urine that has a deep yellow or orange color, indicates fluid depletion. A volume of 2.0 liters of very lightly colored urine indicates high fluid intake.

Fluid depletion has many physical manifestations. With a 2% fluid deficit, individuals may experience mental deterioration, discomfort, lack of energy and appetite, flushed skin, sleeplessness, nausea, and an increased pulse rate.

Inability to swallow, swollen tongue, sunken eyes, and decreased neurological balance occur with a 12% fluid deficit. Should the deficit reach 15%, potentially lethal problems may develop. Delirium, vision disturbances, and shriveled skin are common.

You can never drink too much fluid while in the wilderness. In fact, even if you *think* you are drinking enough, you are probably not. The easiest way to replace lost fluids is to drink more. Most nonalcoholic beverages are suitable, and since water contains no electrolytes, fruit juices, some soft drinks, and fluid replacement drinks are encouraged. Avoid caffeinated beverages, however, as they contain diuretic agents (caffeine) that increase fluid loss through the kidneys.

Thirst is a poor indicator of hydration. If you feel thirsty, you are already dehydrated. Keep one step ahead of dehydration, and the accompanying heat illnesses, by drinking copiously and frequently throughout the day. **Drink, Drink, Drink!!!**

SUNBURN

Sunburn is a real concern for climbers. Each 1000-foot increase in altitude increases the intensity of sunburn-producing ultraviolet light by 4%. Water reflects nearly 100% when the sun is directly overhead; fresh snow reflects 70–90% of ultraviolet light. Reflected sunlight is often more damaging than direct sunlight because it strikes areas of the skin that are normally unexposed, untanned, and unprotected—under the chin, the roof of the mouth, and inside the nose.

Regular use of sunscreens prevent premature aging and lessens the likelihood of eventual skin cancer development. Sunscreen should be applied to all exposed areas with sufficient frequency to be effective. Apply at least 1 hour prior to exposure to allow time for the sunscreen to bond with the skin.

Climbers should use a waterproof sunscreen with an SPF (Sun Protection Factor) of at least 15. The SPF is the ratio of time required to produce the same degree of redness through a sunscreen compared to the time required to produce the same degree of redness without the sunscreen. With SPF 15, if you normally would burn in 1 hour without it, it will now take you 15 hours to obtain the same degree of burn.

Mild sunburns can be treated simply with aspirin and medicated sunburn spray, while more severe burns should be treated like a thermal burn, and may require a visit to the doctor. Of course, prevention is clearly the treatment of choice. *You will not prevent a tan by applying sunscreen, only prevent a burn.*

QUICK CARE

HEAT CRAMPS
- [ ] Assessment
  - ○ Mild tingling in muscles at start
  - ○ Progress to severe, incapacitating pain
  - ○ Nausea
  - ○ Pale, cool, moist skin
- [ ] Treatment
  - ○ Get out of the sun
  - ○ Administer liquids
  - ○ Do not rub cramps
  - ○ Take rest of day off

HEAT RESPONSE
- [ ] Assessment
  - ○ Removes clothes
  - ○ Seeks shade
  - ○ Increases Fluid Replacement
- [ ] Treatment
  - ○ Continue to maximize heat loss
  - ○ Hydration

HEAT EXHAUSTION
- [ ] Assessment
  - ○ Headache ○ Nausea ○ Vomiting ○ Fainting
  - ○ Pale, cool, clammy skin ○ Disorientation
  - ○ Rapid pulse/respiration ○ Thirst
- [ ] Treatment
  - ○ Get out of sun immediately
  - ○ Replace lost fluids
  - ○ Cool body to lower temperature
  - ○ Hospital

HEAT STROKE (HYPERTHERMIA)

- ☐ Assessment
  - ○ Confusion
  - ○ Delirium
  - ○ Hot, dry skin
  - ○ Rapid pulse/respiration
- ☐ Treatment
  - ○ Get out of sun immediately
  - ○ Remove clothes
  - ○ Aggressively cool body
  - ○ If alert, give liquids
  - ○ Immediate evacuation

SUNBURN

- ☐ Avoid prolonged exposure to sun
- ☐ Wear SPF of at least 15
- ☐ Aspirin and spray for mild burns
- ☐ Serious burns require medical attention

10
COLD INJURIES

My first experience with hypothermia was during a season I never expected it would strike—summer. It was probably 100 °F in the valley below Windy Point on Mount Lemmon, AZ, and a good 80 °F where I was climbing. My party and I were doing a pinnacle climb, and I worked up quite a sweat leading it. As I waited on top, belaying the rest of the party, a thunderstorm started developing over the mountains. The wind picked up, and I started to shiver. As the storm moved closer, the temperature began to drop and a slow drizzle started. By the time the last of the party had summited, I was shivering so hard I could hardly move. I needed help setting up my rappel, and I almost tripped going over the side. By the time I reached the ground, I had a full-blown case of mild hypothermia—in the heat of the summer desert.

Hypothermia is a killer. Striking quickly and suddenly, it knows no seasons. Hypothermia is serious, and should always be considered a threat when playing in the outdoors.

Frostbite, as well, should be taken seriously. It is not uncommon for climbers, albeit mostly alpine climbers, to lose fingers, toes, or the tip of a nose. You may never expect to be in a situation where frostbite is a concern, but you never know when a freak snowstorm might trap you at your favorite crag.

Both hypothermia and frostbite are simple to prevent, but harder to treat. By knowing the mechanisms that contribute to the development of each, the identifying symptoms, and the proper treatments, cold injuries should never end your climbing career.

HOW YOUR BODY LOSES HEAT

Recall from Chapter 9 that, in the human body, there are essentially four ways of losing vital heat: radiation, evaporation, convection, and conduction. There are, however, two additional ways the body loses heat in cold weather: through respiration and contact with cold objects.

Every breath of air that you take must be warmed and humidified by the body. In cold temperatures, this air is warmed to body temperature and moistened to 100% humidity by the heat and moisture in your respiratory system. At higher elevations, where the decrease in oxygen concentration requires deeper breathing, more energy is expended in the respiration process. Experts estimate that at these higher elevations, as much as 2300 kilocalories and 4 liters of water are lost daily as the body makes attempts to heat inspired air.

The body also looses heat through contact with cold objects. Water, snow, rocks, gear, or other cold objects are great conductors of heat. Climbing on a cold day can accelerate the release of heat from your body through contact with the rock and metal gear that has been exposed to the elements.

Radiation: Occurs when heat is transferred from a hot to a cold object without direct contact. A hatless head is an excellent heat radiator.

Evaporation: Occurs normally through sweating and breathing.

Convection: Occurs as heat is lost to moving water or air.

Conduction: Occurs as heat is transferred through direct contact of a hot with a cold object, as by leaning your warm body against a cool rock.

HOW HEAT LOSS OCCURS

HYPOTHERMIA

Hypothermia occurs when the body releases more heat than it can produce. This heat loss occurs over time, and can be attributed to a combination of the above mentioned factors.

The normal body temperature of a climber is 98.6°F. At an ambient (still air) temperature of 82°F, an unclothed human body loses more heat to the environment than it can generate *or* retain. Contrary to popular belief, hypothermia is not restricted to cold days, and can occur when the temperature is at its highest. Recall that one precaution in cooling a *hyperthermic* patient is to be on the watch for the development of hypothermia.

Hypothermia can generally be divided into two forms: mild and severe.

MILD HYPOTHERMIA

WHAT YOU SEE

Recognition is the key to warding off the onset of mild hypothermia.

Persons with mild hypothermia generally have a core body temperature between 90.0°F–98.6°F and demonstrate some muscular incoordination.

The most apparent early warning of hypothermia is feeling cold. Shivering and painfully cold feet and hands all indicate the onset of hypothermia. Shivering is the body's way of producing heat, and the feeling of cold in the extremities is due to the shunting of blood away from these areas in response to a reduction in core body temperature. Shivering generally occurs when a drop of 2°F–4°F in the body's core temperature has occurred.

In the early stages of hypothermia, the climber exhibits these signs and symptoms: **chilled feeling & "goose" bumps** **numb skin** These progress to: **shivering** **apathy & slow/improper** **responses** **clumsiness (stiff, clumsy fingers)** **EARLY STAGES OF HYPOTHERMIA**	In the late stages of hypothermia, the climber exhibits these signs and symptoms: **stumbling & falling** **irrational behavior** **incoherence/mental deterioration** **unconsciousness** **LATE STAGES OF HYPOTHERMIA**

As mild hypothermia progresses, intellectual functions become impaired; personality changes, irritability, and the refusal to admit that something is wrong are typical of the hypothermic patient. Mental sluggishness becomes apparent, and the person may become unconcerned or apathetic about their condition.

Often more noticeable is a decrease in the motor abilities of the patient. If hiking, the climber may stumble about, lagging far behind the group, and generally show signs of incoordination. In a climbing situation, these signs may become apparent as the climber attempts to set up rappels and anchors. Gear may be dropped, the individual may seem confused as to procedures, and safety guidelines might be ignored.

WHAT YOU DO

The main concern when treating a mildly hypothermic climber is minimizing further heat loss. This can be accomplished by putting on more clothing: sweaters, socks, mittens, sweats, windbreakers, or whatever is available. Replace wet clothing if possible, and seek protection from the elements. Caves, trees, and manmade shelters all

FIELD TREATMENT OF HYPOTHERMIA
You can minimize heat loss by adding warm, dry clothing, creating a shelter from the elements, and eating some food.

work well in preventing heat loss from the wind. Stemming the flow of heat from your partner's body is critical.

Since it is likely that you will be climbing within hiking distance from your car, once you have adequately reduced heat loss, start hiking back. A large amount of heat can be generated by exercising the large muscles in the legs and back.

Finally, give the hypothermic individual some food. The body's heat-producing and retaining mechanisms cannot work without energy. Food with a high carbohydrate content is best in these circumstances, since carbohydrates are processed quickly by the body. Nuts, dried fruits, candies, power bars, and "gorp" or "trail mix" will all do the job.

Unless you suspect that the climber is bordering on severe hypothermia, there is no need for a hospital visit. Getting the individual to a warm environment is crucial. Once mild hypothermia has been corrected, refrain from returning the person to the same environment without additional protection. Although the individual may appear recovered, his energy stores are low and his body will have a hard time fighting the onset of a new case of hypothermia. Warm up and take the day off.

SEVERE HYPOTHERMIA

WHAT YOU SEE

Persons with severe hypothermia experience internal temperatures below 90°F, exhibit severe intellectual and muscular impairment, and may be unconscious.

The first indicator of severe hypothermia is the reduction in shivering. At this point, the body has used its energy stores and shivering is no longer possible. Additionally, muscular incoordination becomes so severe that the person often cannot walk by themselves, and may not even be able to stand without support.

Intellectual diminution becomes more severe. Disregard for protection from the cold often occurs, as where the individual leaves jackets unzipped, gloves off, and hoods down. Gross errors in judgement are made, contributing to the decline of the hypothermic individual.

Eventually, if left untreated, these signs will progress to incoherence, semiconsciousness, and, finally, total unconsciousness. The patient will not respond to any stimulus, and will appear to be in a coma. Breathing and heart rates may become so shallow and slow that they often appear absent (6 beats per minute and 10 respirations per minute are not uncommon). *No one should be considered cold and dead until they have been warm and dead!!!*

WHAT YOU DO

Severely hypothermic patients need to be rewarmed. As a climber in the field, there is little you can do to rewarm the patient adequately. Your first goal should be to obtain help for this individual. Send a member of your group to get professional help, or, if you are by yourself, make efforts to warm the patient *externally*, and then go for help.

Begin by making efforts to dry the patient, replacing any wet clothing with dry ones. If you are exposed to the elements, find a warm, dry place to be, out of the wind. Build a shelter if nothing exists. Minimize contact with anything that is colder than the patient, as such contact will increase the loss of heat through conduction.

Severely hypothermic patients often experience a life-threatening condition called ventricular fibrillation. This occurs when all the muscle cells of the heart contract independently, leaving the heart unable to pump blood.

Movement, even the slightest movements, can cause a severely hypothermic individual's heart to go into ventricular fibrillation. Thus, it is extremely important that you minimize movement of such a person. Again, obtaining professional medical assistance is your most crucial task in this situation.

PREVENTION OF HYPOTHERMIA

The best way to prevent becoming a victim of hypothermia is to never allow yourself to get too cold. This may not be a concern when you are actively pumping the rocks, but the moment you sit down to rest, your body begins to cool, and your temperature drops. A concern in all seasons, you should be prepared to stay warm whatever the outside temperature.

Given that many climbers of are the skinny type, with little body fat, we are particularly susceptible to hypothermia. Climbers with little insulating body fat, particularly males, have a hard time maintaining the proper temperature balance.

When preparing for your climbing trip, even if it is only a day trip, it is important to consider the possibility of hypothermia. Always carry waterproof external garments in the event that the weather deteriorates, and use them immediately if it does. At the very least, carry a windbreaker. Wind chill contributes greatly to the decline in body temperature through convection.

Wear clothing in layers. Each successive layer should be larger than the one beneath it. Allow a quarter of an inch between the layers; if they are the same size, the insulation quality of the clothing is lost. Avoid cotton clothing; wool has traditionally been chosen for its outstanding insulating properties, even when wet. There are a myriad of outdoor clothes on the market that should protect you in any situation. Avoid the "death uniform"—cotton jeans and a T-shirt.

Remember to eat and drink frequently. Your body needs energy to keep itself warm (or cool). It is better to eat food at frequent intervals, thus preventing the depletion of energy stores and keeping a consistent level of energy throughout the day. Water is important as well. Dehydration decreases blood volume, impairs heat production by exercise, and increases the risk of frostbite due to constriction of the blood in the extremities. Mild exertion requires at least 2 quarts of water per day, while 3–5 quarts is needed for heavier exertion or at high altitudes. *You can never drink too much!!*

FROSTBITE

Frostbite occurs when the tissues of the body have been frozen. The hands and feet, the ears, and the face, particularly the tip of the nose, are the most commonly afflicted areas.

As the body begins to get cold, it restricts blood flow to the extremities to conserve heat. As circulation diminishes in these areas, and heat is lost in the tissues, they begin to freeze. Ice crystals form within and between the cells and grow by extracting water from inside the cells. This freezing does not necessarily kill the cells, but permanent damage from improper rewarming can result.

The chances of becoming frostbitten increase if there is a high wind in addition to low temperatures. Wind increases the wind chill factor, which in effect decreases the temperature. For example, if it is -50°F outside with a 40 mph wind, the equivalent wind chill temperature would be -132°F. This dramatic increase in temperature contributes to the problems of protecting yourself from frostbite.

WHAT YOU SEE

The early signs of frostbite are cold, pain, and pallor (whiteness) in the affected tissues. As freezing progresses, the tissues become increasingly whiter, and all sensation is lost, including pain. Extremities with extensive frostbite, such as feet and hands, often exhibit a dull purple color.

The extent of frostbite is often difficult to diagnose until the healing process has begun. Minor frostbite produces redness and swelling that lasts for a few days but leaves no permanent damage.

Blisters develop after rewarming on extremities that have been more severely injured. If the blisters contain clear fluid, the underlying tissue can be expected to recover. When the blisters contain bloody fluid, the underlying tissue should not be expected to recover, and the extremity may be lost. With digits, if the clear blisters do not cover the tips of the digit, the uncovered area

WIND CHILL CHART

TEMPERATURE °F

WIND SPEED (MPH)	50	40	30	20	10	0	-10	-20	-30
	EQUIVALENT CHILL TEMPERATURE °F								
Calm	50	40	30	20	10	0	-10	-20	-30
5	48	37	27	16	6	-5	-15	-26	-36
10	40	28	16	4	-9	-21	-33	-46	-58
15	36	22	9	-5	-18	-36	-45	-58	-72
20	32	18	4	-10	-25	-39	-53	-67	-82
25	30	16	0	-15	-29	-44	-59	-74	-88
30	28	13	-2	-18	-33	-48	-63	-79	-94
35	27	11	-4	-20	-35	-51	-67	-82	-98
40	26	10	-6	-21	-37	-53	-69	-85	-100

Over 40 mph adds little to the effect

Little Danger of freezing exposed flesh if properly clothed & dry	Great Danger of exposed flesh freezing	Extreme Danger of exposed flesh freezing

will eventually be lost.

After a week to 10 days, frostbitten tissues develop a thick, black covering called "eschar." After 4 to 6 weeks, this dead tissue, including entire fingers or toes, will separate spontaneously.

WHAT YOU DO

The preferred treatment for frostbite is rapid rewarming in a water bath. Since there is no way to accomplish this in the field, evacuate the frostbitten individual to a hospital. In the meantime, take precautions to prevent further exposure to the elements, and ensure that the rest of the body remains warm.

One word of warning. While it is human nature to rub body parts when they are cold, do not do so when frostbite is suspected. Rubbing tissues that have intracellular ice crystals in them can cause tissue damage. Rapid rewarming is the most effective treatment, and it cannot be carried out adequately by most people in the field. Seek professional help.

QUICK CARE

HYPOTHERMIA

Mild

- ☐ Assessment
  - ○ Feeling cold
  - ○ Painfully cold feet/hands
  - ○ Irritability
  - ○ Decrease in motor abilities
  - ○ Shivering
  - ○ Personality changes
  - ○ Mental sluggishness
- ☐ Treatment
  - ○ Minimize further heat loss
  - ○ Replace wet clothes
  - ○ Evacuate to warm environment
  - ○ Administer food, liquids

Severe

- ☐ Assessment
  - ○ Reduction in shivering
  - ○ Severe muscular incoordination
  - ○ Disregard for personal safety
  - ○ Gross errors in judgement
  - ○ Decreased levels of consciousness
  - ○ Absence of pulse/respiration
- ☐ Treatment
  - ○ Warm externally
  - ○ Protect from environment
  - ○ Seek professional assistance
  - ○ Replace wet clothing
  - ○ Minimize movement

FROSTBITE

- ☐ Assessment
  - ○ Cold
  - ○ Loss of sensation
  - ○ Blister after rewarming
  - ○ Pain
  - ○ Pallor
  - ○ Dull, purple color
- ☐ Treatment
  - ○ Professional rewarming in water bath

11
ALTITUDE ILLNESS

*In May of 1992, a solo Korean climber, camped at Denali Pass (18,200')
on Mt. McKinley, developed a serious case of Acute Mountain Sickness and
High Altitude Pulmonary Edema. Over the next 2 days, the climber was
evacuated to 14,200' by rescue team members. On the third day, he was air
evacuated to a hospital, where it was discovered that he had severe frostbite
to both hands and pneumonia complicated by High Altitude Pulmonary
Edema. Later analysis determined that most of the climber's problems might
have been avoided had he acclimatized to the region before beginning his
climb, and had he recognized the symptoms of Acute Mountain Sickness and
High Altitude Pulmonary Edema.*

Alright, so most of us will never climb at the high altitudes encountered
on mountains like K2 and Mt. McKinley. Nevertheless, there are many
climbing crags across the states at altitudes above 8,000', the definition of high
altitude. Since most climbers do not allow themselves time to get used to an
unfamiliar altitude before they climb, it is important to understand the basics
of altitude illness.

There are essentially three divisions in defining what high altitudes are:
High Altitude (8,000–14,000 feet), Very High Altitude (14,000–18,000 feet) and
Extremely High Altitude (above 18,000 feet).

ALTITUDE AND THE BODY

Humans need oxygen to live. As we breath, oxygen from the environment
passes through our lungs, eventually reaching tiny structures called alveoli.
At this point, oxygen is diffused from the alveoli into the bloodstream,
distributed, and fed to the tissues of the body. At normal altitudes, 8,000 feet
and below, this is a relatively easy process. The gas pressure is greater in the
alveoli than in the bloodstream and diffusion is readily accomplished.

As climbers move up in altitude, the amount of oxygen in the air stays the
same, a habitable 21%, but the air pressure decreases. This reduction in air
pressure also brings about a decrease in the air density, which means that with
each breath you bring in fewer oxygen molecules than before. Thus, an
increase in your respiratory rate is a first sign that your body is responding to

an oxygen crisis.

Every organ in the body is sensitive to the amounts of oxygen it receives, though some are less tolerant of a reduction in oxygen than others. The brain is perhaps the quickest to complain when acceptable levels of oxygen saturation are not being met.

Since the brain consumes some 20% of all the oxygen that the body brings in, a decrease in its normal levels prompts it to respond by sending more blood to the area. This influx of blood fills the already cramped confines of the skull, causing the brain to swell, and that swelling precedes one of the most obvious signs of altitude illness—a headache. If the swelling is allowed to progress without some relief, which can be obtained by a speedy descent, a condition known as High Altitude Cerebral Edema (HACE) can develop.

The most active place in the body where blood becomes oxygenated is in the lungs. As a climber progresses in altitude, and the oxygen level of the blood decreases, the body responds by sending more blood into the lungs. This increase in blood volume often results in a leakage of fluid out of the blood vessels and into the air spaces. Left untreated, this condition develops into High Altitude Pulmonary Edema (HAPE). The flow of fluid into the air spaces make an already obstructed system even more so, and the body's oxygen debt becomes worse.

Any outdoor participant who plays in altitudes over 8,000 feet should be aware of the signs and symptoms of the three major types of altitude illnesses: Acute Mountain Sickness (AMS), High Altitude Cerebral Edema (HACE), and High Altitude Pulmonary Edema (HAPE).

ACUTE MOUNTAIN SICKNESS (AMS)

Acute Mountain Sickness applies to a group of symptoms that generally occur in unacclimatized people who make rapid ascents to above 8,000 feet, such as the weekend skier who flies in from sea level, or people who partially acclimatize and then make an abrupt ascent to a higher altitude.

WHAT YOU SEE

Signs and symptoms of AMS begin to present themselves around 6 to 72 hours after arrival at high altitude, and usually disappear within 2 to 6 days. Symptoms include headache, general malaise (uneasy feeling), loss of appetite, nausea and vomiting, peripheral edema (fluid retention in face and hands), disturbed sleep, and cyanosis of the fingernail beds, mucous membranes, and the mouth.

What You Do

Limit activities above 8,000 feet for the first 3 days and allow yourself time to acclimatize. Drink plenty of water to maintain hydration (a problem at altitude), and get plenty of rest. Aspirin, acetaminophen, or ibuprofen may ease the headache. However, as at sea level, do not use these in excess.

Should symptoms persist or become worse, descend to where they first occurred and spend more time acclimatizing. Usually a descent of 2,000 to 3,000 feet is sufficient.

High Altitude Cerebral Edema (HACE)

High Altitude Cerebral Edema (HACE) is swelling of the brain which happens as the body rushes to get more oxygenated blood into the brain. HACE generally occurs above 12,000 feet, but has been recorded at lower altitudes.

What You See

The classic signs of HACE are presence of AMS, change in level of consciousness, ataxia, vision disturbances, paralysis, seizures, hallucinations, and cyanosis. Ataxia is evident in the legs and feet first, then in the arms and hands. Individuals may have problems holding objects such as a cup, and may also slip in and out of various levels of consciousness.

What You Do

There is only one treatment for HACE: **DESCEND!!** and seek immediate medical help. Waiting for the symptoms to subside may result in the climber's death. Descend to a lower elevation the moment you notice signs of ataxia or a change in the climbers level of consciousness. Waste no time in seeking professional medical help.

High Altitude Pulmonary Edema (HAPE)

High Altitude Pulmonary Edema occurs when fluid leaks out of the excess blood that has accumulated in the lungs as a result of the increased oxygen demand. HAPE is more common in young males, and generally occurs at altitudes above 8,000 feet.

What You See

The symptoms of HAPE start to present themselves 24–96 hours after ascent to altitude. Symptoms include signs of AMS, shortness of breath with exertion leading to shortness of breath, general fatigue, a dry cough progressing to a wet cough with phlegm, increased heart and respiratory rates, fluid sounds in the lungs (rales), and ataxia (loss of muscle coordination).

As HAPE worsens, climbing and breathing become more and more difficult. Weakness and fatigue occur when walking on level ground. Symptoms may appear like the flu or bronchitis.

In severe HAPE, the respiratory rate exceeds 30 breaths/minute and a heart rate greater than 110 beats/minute. Cyanosis can be observed in the fingernail beds and in the face. The patient may begin to cough up frothy blood-tinged phlegm. The individual becomes more ataxic and lethargic, often unconscious.

WHAT YOU DO

HAPE is a life-threatening illness and must be treated immediately. The victim must be lowered in altitude as quickly as possible—2,000 to 3,000 feet at a minimum. Continue to descend until the symptoms begin to subside.

A climber who has been afflicted with mild HAPE should seek medical attention as soon as possible. If none is available, the affected climber should not engage in any physical activity for a minimum of 3 days, to allow the fluid in the lungs to be reabsorbed. If an attempt to ascend is tried again, observe the patient for a relapse.

PREVENTION OF ALTITUDE ILLNESSES

As with many medical problems in the wilderness, recognition is still the key factor in preventing a serious case of altitude illness from developing.

First and foremost, learning to recognize the signs and symptoms of AMS are extremely important. Climbers are often a stubborn bunch, many of whom push themselves past discomfort and deny symptoms that may be associated with AMS. By the time the problem has progressed to the point they cannot physically continue, the altitude illness has reached a critical level.

The surest and safest method of preventing altitude illness is to make a slow, graded ascent. Avoid abrupt ascent to sleeping altitudes greater than 10,000 feet and average no more than 1,000 feet of elevation gain per day at altitudes over 10,000 feet. Taking day trips to higher altitudes and returning to lower altitudes for sleep will aid in acclimatization.

Your diet at altitude should consist of foods high in carbohydrates and low in fat. As important is remembering to stay hydrated—**Drink, Drink, Drink!!!**

There are some over-the-counter drugs that can be used to help forestall altitude illness, and also to help treat altitude illness once it has developed. Drugs should not be used as a substitute for a graded ascent in any condition.

Diamox (acetazolamide) is a prescription drug that may help prevent altitude illness when used in conjunction with a slow ascent. Diamox works by increasing your respiration rate, which ultimately decreases the oxygen debt in your body. On the down side, Diamox is a diuretic, which means that your urine output will increase. Drink copiously.

Two other drugs—Nifedipine and Decadron (dexamethasone)—can be used for the treatment of HAPE and HACE, respectively. These drugs should only be taken under the direction of a qualified individual, and should only be used once symptoms of altitude illness have been observed. Neither of these drugs promote acclimatization to altitude.

Remember that all drugs should be obtained through a physician's prescription and the effects and use of each should be fully understood before their application.

Finally, if there is one available, place the patient in a Gamow Bag. This bag simulates a decrease in atmospheric pressure, and afflicted individuals placed in one generally show marked improvement within hours. Use of this bag should also be done under trained supervision. While the Gamow Bag will not prevent altitude illnesses from developing, it's use will go a long way in preventing the climber from getting worse.

The exact mechanisms that cause one climber to be affected by altitude and not another are poorly understood. Currently, there is nothing to indicate that fitness level has anything to do in deciding who gets sick and who feels fine. If any of the above-described symptoms should occur when at altitude, the best course of action is to assume that an altitude-related problem is developing, and take steps to correct it.

Should you ever forget what the exact symptoms of an altitude illness are, keep in mind this quote from British climber Edward Whymper in 1876:

"I found myself flat on my back . . . incapable of making even the least exertion. We were experiencing our first attack of mountain sickness. We had intense headaches and were unable to satisfy our desire for air. . . . The headaches for all three of us were so intense and rendered us almost frantic or crazy."

QUICK CARE

ACUTE MOUNTAIN SICKNESS (AMS)

☐ Assessment
  - ○ Headache   ○ General malaise   ○ Loss of appetite
  - ○ Nausea   ○ Vomiting   ○ Peripheral edema
  - ○ Disturbed sleep   ○ Cyanosis

☐ Treatment
  - ○ Limit activities above 8000' (2400 meters) for first 3 days
  - ○ Keep hydrated

HIGH ALTITUDE CEREBRAL EDEMA (HACE)

☐ Assessment
  - ○ AMS
  - ○ Changes in level of consciousness
  - ○ Ataxia   ○ Vision disturbances   ○ Paralysis
  - ○ Seizures   ○ Hallucinations

☐ Treatment
  - ○ Descend immediately and seek professional help

HIGH ALTITUDE PULMONARY EDEMA (HAPE)

☐ Assessment
  - ○ Signs of AMS
  - ○ Shortness of breath
  - ○ Dry cough progressing to wet cough
  - ○ Increased pulse/respiration
  - ○ Fluid sounds in lungs
  - ○ Ataxia

☐ Treatment
  - ○ Descend until symptoms subside
  - ○ Seek medical help

12
SHORT DISTANCE TRANSFER

*Cathedral Ledge in New Hampshire was the scene of a climbing accident in October 1993. Two climbers were doing a four pitch route called **Diedre** on a chilly Fall day. Moving into a sequence that involved a large crack, the leader found himself in a perilous position as his body weakened from the days' climbing and the impending cold. Soon, he had fallen some 10 to 12 feet, with a slight pendulum, hitting the bony protrusion on the side of his knee. Initial attempts at walking on the knee were unsuccessful, and his partner (5'6", 130 lbs.) wound up carrying him 300 feet to the road. The injury proved to be a fracture of the left tibia, requiring a 2-hour operation and four titanium screws.*

If you spend enough time in the wilderness, it is almost certain there will be a time when you are required to carry someone a short distance, whether to shelter or to safety. If Murphy's Law continues to work as it has for centuries, the person you will have to carry will weigh twice as much as you, and will be a good foot taller. Not to dismay, there are ways to effectively and safely move anyone in the wilderness.

In considering short distance transfers, the use of available materials will be emphasized. Since you are a climber, you will (hopefully) have in your possession at least one rope and numerous pieces of webbing. Necessity being the mother of invention, these items are very effective in moving an injured climber a short distance. Additionally, a simple drag is useful in moving a climber out of imminent danger.

This chapter illustrates transfer methods that can be used by one to four climbers.

DRAGS

The only time that you will want to drag an injured climber is if she must be moved quickly out of danger—falling rock, severe cold or winds, blowing snow, and water for example. As always, it is important to assess the climber *before* attempting a drag, because some injuries may be aggravated by such a maneuver. Should it be necessary to perform a drag to move an injured climber, it is important to observe the following precautions:

1. **Drag headfirst.** This allows you to support the climber's head and neck and keep her body straight.

2. **Keep the body in-line.** Avoid twisting or bending the body, and avoid bumps.

3. **Support the head and neck.** Do not allow the neck to bend sharply or fall from side-to-side.

To drag a climber, reach under her body and grip her clothing just below the shoulder level on either side of the body, so that your forearms support her head and neck. Stay in a kneeling or crouched position as you drag the climber backwards. Be careful not to injure your back in the process!

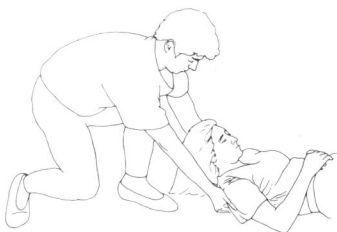

DRAGGING BY GRIPPING CLOTHING

DRAGGING BY TARP

If possible, secure the injured climber's hands together before dragging to protect them. A piece of webbing works nicely for this, as does cuff buttons or Velcro.

If you have a tarp, this will greatly aid in the drag process. Log-roll (explained later in this chapter) the patient onto the tarp, grip the tarp in such a way that her head and shoulders are off the ground, and drag carefully. Leaving the tarp under the climber may help aid rescuers if they need to lift her into a litter.

ROPE COIL CARRY

If the injured climber is conscious, the rope coil carry is an excellent way to transport the climber who has minor injuries. To begin, make a rope coil about 2 feet long, fasten with a tight wrap, and split into two equal parts.

Have the climber place a leg through each half. Crouch down and place the coils over your shoulders as you would do if putting on a backpack. Rise, using your legs to do the work. If needed, pad all areas that are uncomfortable with extra clothing, or whatever is available.

Be aware that the rope coil carry, while somewhat comfortable, has the action of reducing the circulation in the climbers legs. Rest often to relieve the pressure, and in severe cold, check for frostbite.

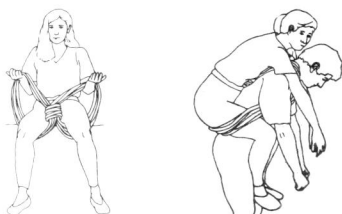

ROPE COIL CARRY

TWO-PERSON ROPE COIL CARRY

Carrying an injured person is always easier if there are two people to split the work. The two-person rope coil carry is effective in that it supports the weight of the patient on the shoulders of the rescuers, and reduces the twisting motion caused by other two person carries using the hands.

To accomplish this carry, begin by making a coil as in the rope coil carry, and split it. Place half of the coil over each rescuer's outside shoulder. The secured area of the coils forms the seat on which the patient will sit. Padding again is very desirable, this time on the areas of the rescuer's shoulders and the patients seat.

Ask the patient to sit in the seat with her arms around the rescuer's shoulders, getting into the most comfortable position before the rescuer's rise from a kneeling position. Your inner hands may be used to support the climbers back, while outer hands remain free.

TWO-PERSON ROPE COIL CARRY

NYLON WEBBING CARRY

Any climber worth his weight in safety carries some nylon webbing with him. This webbing can be extremely valuable in concocting a system by which a mildly injured climber can be carried for small distances with minimal discomfort. Remember to pad the nylon very well at every point it presses against the body, especially under the climber's thighs, where concentrated pressure will cause a loss of circulation.

The nylon webbing carry is a back carry, and is best described in the following illustration.

Step 1:
Around the patient

Step 2:
Around the carrier

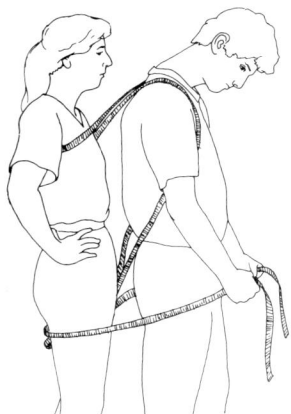

Step 3:
Around the thighs

Step 4:
Lifting

Step 5:
Carrying

NYLON WEBBING CARRY

LOG-ROLL AND FOUR-PERSON CARRY

There may be times when a patient that is suspected of having a back or neck injury must be moved a short distance for whatever reason; perhaps to place insulation between the patient and the ground, or to remove the patient from harms way. In the event that movement becomes necessary, knowledge of both the log-roll and the four-person carry are helpful.

In performing a log-roll on an injured patient, the key is to maintain the alignment of both the neck and spine. Any unnecessary movement could further exacerbate any damage that has been done, potentially resulting in paralysis or even death.

At all times during the movement the patient's head and back must be kept in straight alignment, and the head should be manually supported until it has been stabilized by some means after the movement has occurred.

Step 1: Place the patient & the pad side-by-side.

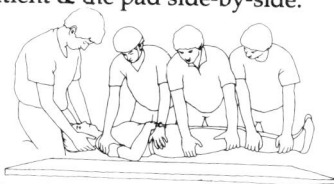

Step 2: Keeping the head in line with the body, turn patient on side and move the pad, not the patient, underneath. Gently roll patient onto pad.

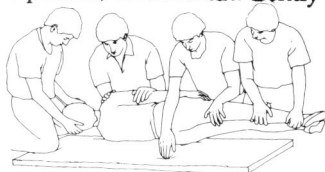

PERFORMING THE LOG-ROLL

The following steps should be followed when performing a log-roll, and should be practiced prior to their use in the field.

1. Designate one member of the party to be the leader, and station that person at the head of the patient. The leader should place his hands on the climbers head, where his fingers are used to support the back of the head and jaw, with the palms covering the ears. The intent here is to prevent movement of the head relative to the rest of the body. Additonally, the leader becomes the source of all commands during the roll.

2. If necessary, provide in-line traction to place the head in a straight line with the rest of the body, as outlined in Chapter 3. Stop movement if resistance or severe pain is encountered.

3. The other rescuers should assume places on one side of the climber's body. One should be located at the shoulders, one near the hips, and a third at the knees. All rescuers should be on their knees.

4. Place the insulation material on the far side of the climber, ready to move under the climber when the roll has been executed.

5. Lift the climber's arm that is on the opposite side of the rescuers out of the way by placing it across the chest, taking care to support the shoulders and back to minimize movement to the spine.

6. The arm located nearest the rescuer should be lifted up and out of the way of the roll, again taking precautions to protect the spine.

7. The rescuer at the shoulder should place one hand under the climber's far shoulder and the second at the top of the hips. The person at the hips places one hand at the middle of the trunk and the second midthigh. The final rescuer places one hand under the knees, the other cradling the ankle.

8. When everyone is in position, the leader calls "Ready to roll," and when all confirm they are ready, "Roll." At this point the victim is slowly rolled towards the rescuer's knees. The rescuer at the hips should then place the insulation material under the climber.

9. Finally, the leader calls "Ready to lower," and then "Lower" when all signify they are ready. The leader remains at the climber's head until it has been stabilized as outlined in Chapter 3.

If it becomes necessary to move the climber a short distance, for whatever reason, a four-person carry can be used. This technique is for short distances

FOUR-PERSON CARRY

only, and should be done with care, and very slowly. The steps are as follows:

1. A leader is nominated and placed at the head in the manner outlined in the log-roll. Straighten the victim's head if necessary.

2. Kneeling on one knee, the other rescuers assume positions on both sides of the climber. The rescuer on the shoulders and the one at the legs are on the same side of the climber.

3. Secure the climber's arms by placing her hands in her waistband, or by lightly tying the hands together.

4. The person at the shoulders gently places one hand under the shoulders and one hand under the hips. The rescuer at the knees places one hand beneath the hips, and the other under the knees. The person stationed at the hips moves one hand under the middle of the back and the other hand under the mid-thigh area.

5. The leader calls "Prepare to lift," and then "Lift" when all are ready. Slowly lift the climber, no more than necessary, and move her forward no more than a few feet. Lower, and repeat the lift sequence until you have reached your final location.

The four-person carry is tedious and slow, but is relatively safe in protecting the injured climber from further back or neck injury. Of course, the ultimate course of action is to leave the climber where found, and take efforts to ensure their safety by preparing shelters, protecting them from the elements or any other threats to their safety.

Finally, remember that short transfer methods are not limited to the described methods. Trees, ice axes, packs, ropes, and a multitude of other objects can be employed when attempting to move a patient. Keep in mind that moving a climber who has a suspected spine or back injury is risky business, and should be avoided unless absolutely necessary.

USING ICE AXES

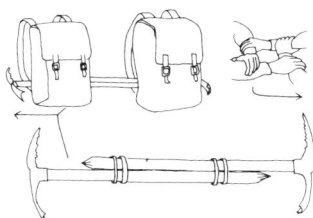

FOUR-HAND SEAT CARRY

QUICK CARE

DRAGS
- ☐ Drag headfirst
- ☐ Keep the body in line
- ☐ Support the head and neck

ROPE COIL CARRY
- ☐ Make a 2' coil with rope
- ☐ Place coils over shoulders
- ☐ Pad areas where coils exert pressure

TWO-PERSON ROPE COIL CARRY
- ☐ Make coil as above
- ☐ Each climber places coil over shoulder
- ☐ Injured climber sits in formed harness

NYLON WEBBING CARRY
- ☐ Use to carry patient on your back
- ☐ Generously pad

LOG-ROLL
- ☐ Maintain alignment of head and spine
- ☐ Designate one rescuer as leader, place at head
- ☐ Roll injured climber as a unit
- ☐ Roll towards rescuers

FOUR-PERSON CARRY
- ☐ Maintain alignment of head and spine
- ☐ Designate one rescuer as leader, place at head
- ☐ Lift vertically no more than necessary
- ☐ Move horizontally no more than a few feet
- ☐ Move climber as a unit

GLOSSARY

A

ABCD's—Airway, Breathing, Circulation, and Disabilities. All are checked and treated during the primary survey.

AEIOUTIPS—Alcohol, Epilepsy, Insulin, Overdose, Underdose, Trauma, Infection, Psychological/Poison, and Stroke. Checked during the secondary survey as possible reasons for the medical problem.

AMS—Acute Mountain Sickness.

AMPLE—Allergies, Medications, Previous History, Last Meal, and Events. Checked during the secondary survey as possible reasons for the medical problem.

AVPU—Alert, Verbal, Pain, Unresponsive. Scale for testing the level of consciousness.

Abrasion—A wound to the skin generally caused by a rubbing or scraping. Sometimes involves the underlying tissue.

Altitude—Vertical height above sea level. Classified as High Altitude (8,000–14,000 feet), Very High Altitude (14,000–18,000 feet), and Extremely High Altitude (above 18,000 feet).

Alveoli—Tiny air cells of the lung.

Amputation—The severing of a limb from the body.

Anatomical Position—Position that the limb is normally found.

Anaphylaxis—A hypersensitive reaction of the body to an allergen.

Ataxia—Loss of muscular coordination; generally found during voluntary movement.

Autonomic Stress Response (ASR)—Condition that mirrors shock, often following sudden stress or injury. Presents as either Sympathetic ASR ("fight or flight") or Parasympathetic ASR (fainting). Associated pain masking often complicates accurate assessment.

Avulsion—A skin injury in which tissue is forcibly torn away or separated.

B

Battle's sign—Bruising behind and at the base of the ears as a result of head trauma.

Bilateral—Two sides; as in bilateral symmetry (the same on both sides).

C

Capillary Refill—The ability of the capillaries under the skin to become perfused with blood once they have been blanched.

Cardiac Arrest—The cessation of heart function; often due to heart disease, trauma, or lightning.

Cardiogenic Shock—Loss of perfusion in the body due to a failure of the pumping mechanism (heart).

Cerebrospinal Fluid—Fluid found in and around the brain.

Circulation—The movement of blood through the vessels of the body as induced by the pumping of the heart.

Concussion—A jarring injury of the brain resulting in a disturbance of cerebral function.

Conduction—Method of heat transfer from direct contact.

Constricted—A closing or shutting of vessels or airways.

Contusion—A bruise.

Crepitus—A grating sound caused by bones rubbing together.

Cyanosis—A purple or bluish discoloration of the lips, nails, and skin that typically results from reduced oxygen in the blood.

Convection—Heat transfer from the motion of two thermally different bodies of air.

D

Death Uniform—Cotton t-shirt and blue jeans. Not advisable to wear when entering the wilderness because of their lack of insulating properties.

Dehydration—Loss of excessive amounts of body fluids (water).

Diabetic Coma—*See* Hyperglycemia.

Dilated—Expanded laterally; pupils that appear very wide, vessels that have expanded in size.

Direct Pressure—The first step in trying to stop bleeding. Pressure should be aimed directly at the visualized wound.

Dislocation—A joint that is not in its normal position.

Distended—Expanded.

E

Edema—Abnormal collection of fluid in the tissues.

Epilepsy—Neurologic disorder characterized by repeated convulsions.

Epinephrine—Drug used in treating anaphylaxis; similar to adrenaline found naturally in the body.

Eschar—Scab formed on burned or frostbitten areas.

F

First Degree Burn—Burn that affects the first layer of skin.

Flail Chest—Chest injury where two or more ribs have been broken in two or more places, causing chest wall instability and paradoxical respiration.

Fracture—Broken bone or cartilage.

Frostbite—Frozen tissue.

G

Gamow Bag—Hyperbaric chamber that simulates descent to a lower altitude and can be used at high altitudes to treat altitude illnesses.

H

HACE—High Altitude Cerebral Edema. Swelling of the brain due to oxygen deprivation at altitude.

HAPE—High Altitude Pulmonary Edema. Swelling of the lung tissue as a result of fluid retention at high altitude.

Head Injury—Injury to the head that involves the brain.

Head Wound—Injury to the head that involves the scalp.

Heat Cramps—Muscle cramps that occur as a result of fluid depletion in the body.

Heat Exhaustion—Sometimes called heat prostration or heat collapse; from significant loss of body fluids through sweating.

Heat Response—Normal body response to a heat challenge.

Heat Stroke—Severe elevation of body temperature (over 105°F).

Hematoma—Collection of blood beneath the skin, forming a lump. Can also occur in spaces like the skull, which increases pressure on the brain.

Hyperglycemia—High concentration of sugar in the blood.

Hypoglycemia—Abnormally low concentration of sugar in the blood.

Hypovolemic (Volume) Shock—Failure of tissue perfusion caused by a deficient fluid volume in the body.

Hypothermia—Abnormally low body temperature, especially in the core.

I

Insulin Shock—State of severe hypoglycemia due to an excessive insulin dose. *See also* Hypoglycemia.

Intercranial Pressure—Pressure within the skull.

L

Laceration—Wound characterized by a ragged cut.

M

Mechanism of Injury—The way in which an injury occurred and the associated forces with it (fall, blunt trauma, glancing blow, etc.).

O

Open Injury—Injury associated with a break in the skin.

P

PFA—Pain Free Activity.

PQRST—Provokes, Quality, Radiation, Severity, and Time. Method for determining the Chief Complaint, and completed during the secondary survey.

Pallor—Whiteness or paleness of the skin.

Parasympathetic ASR—Subset of ASR that is characterized by fainting and nausea. Results from limited perfusion in the blood due to a slow pulse rate.

Pericardium—Fibrous sack that surrounds the heart.

Phlegm—Mucous secreted from the respiratory passages.

Pleura—Double membrane surrounding the lungs.

Pneumothorax—Air in the pleural space.

Primary Survey—The first step in a complete survey of the patient. Includes assessing the scene, checking the ABCD's, treating life-threatening bleeding, and treating for shock.

Pressure Point—Point where an artery lies close to the skin.

Pulse—A regular throbbing caused in the arteries by the contractions of the heart.

Pulmonary Embolism—Clots or globules of fat that have become lodged in the blood vessels of the lungs.

Puncture—Penetration of the skin (and possibly underlying organs) by a pointed object.

R

RICE—Rest, Ice, Compression, and Elevation.

Raccoon's Sign—Bruising under the eyes as a result of head trauma.

Radiation—Emission of heat into the surrounding cold air.

Rales—Abnormal respiratory sounds, having a crackling or bubbling quality, that indicate fluid in the alveoli.

Reduction—Restoration of a broken bone or joint to its proper position.

Respiration—The act of breathing.

S

SPF—Sun Protection Factor. Ratio of time required to produce the same degree of redness through a sunscreen as compared to the amount of time required to produce the same degree of redness without the sunscreen.

Second Degree Burn—Burn that involves both the top and middle layers of the skin.

Secondary Survey—Complete head-to-toe survey completed after the primary survey. Injuries are treated when they are found, and a complete medical history is obtained.

Seizure—Attack of violent muscle contractions.

Shock—State of inadequate tissue perfusion.

Sprain—Injury involving the incomplete rupture of ligaments.

Strain—Injury involving the stretching, with or without tearing, of ligaments or muscles.

Sternum—Breastbone.

Spontaneous Pneumothorax—Pneumothorax occurring without trauma, largely due to a congenital weak area of the lung.

Sympathetic ASR—"Fight or flight" response that often occurs during times of intense stress or trauma. Involves release of hormones that act to mask pain.

T

Tendinitis—Inflammation of a tendon, usually due to repeated movements.

Tension Pneumothorax—Pneumothorax in which air collects in the pleural space under progressively increasing pressure.

Third degree Burn—Burns that destroy all the layers of the skin, and may involve muscle as well.

Tourniquet—A device applied circumferentially to a limb to impede or exclude blood flow to the limb.

V

Vascular (Neurogenic) Shock—Failure of tissue perfusion caused by massive dilation of blood vessels due to failure of nervous control.

Venom—Poisonous substance produced by a snake, spider, etc.

Ventricular Fibrillation—Form of cardiac arrest in which the individual muscle fibers of the heart contract chaotically.

Vital Signs—Level of consciousness on AVPU scale, pulse rate, respiration rate, skin signs, capillary refill time.

APPENDIX
FIRST AID KIT

If you go climbing, you need a first aid kit. Since most of your climbing is going to be done at crags that are near the road, you don't need to take a lot with you. However, there are some items that need to be in your pack when you climb. There are several first aid pack shells that are available on the market for stowing these items, or, if you like the simplistic approach, many can fit in a ziplock bag.

- ☐ 4 – 4"x4" sterile gauze pads
- ☐ 1 – 5"x9" sterile dressing
- ☐ 10 – 1" fabric bandage
- ☐ 2 – 2" roller gauze (Kurlex)
- ☐ 1 – Ace bandage
- ☐ 1 – SAM splint
- ☐ 1 – Sheet Moleskin
- ☐ 4 – Safety pins
- ☐ 1 – Needle (sewing kind best with sewing kit)
- ☐ 1 – Single edged razor
- ☐ 1 – Small scissors
- ☐ 1 – Tweezers
- ☐ 2 – Ziplock bags (medium or large)
- ☐ 2 – Pairs latex gloves (absolutely essential in treating any injury that may involve blood or fluids—ALWAYS PROTECT YOURSELF FIRST).
- ☐ 1 – CPR Shield or Pocket Mask (makes artificial respiration much easier and safer).
- ☐ 4 – Antibiotic ointment (Neosporin, Tribiotic, etc).
- ☐ 10 – Analgesic tablets (Motrin, aspirin, Tylenol, Advil).
- ☐ 1 – Pencil or pen
- ☐ 1 – Small notebook (or report form such as those found on pages 410–411 of *Mountaineering: Freedom of the Hills, 5th Edition.*)
- ☐ 1 – Duct tape wrapped around writing instrument (for securing splints, immobilization, bandages, etc.)

REFERENCES

Caroline, N.L. *Emergency Medical Treatment: Third Edition*. Boston: Little, Brown, and Company, 1991.

Darvill, F.T. *Mountaineering Medicine: A Wilderness Medical Guide*. Seattle: Wilderness Press, 1992.

Goth, P., and J. Isaac. *The Outward Bound Wilderness First-Aid Handbook*. New York: Lyons and Burford, 1991.

Graydon, D. *Mountaineering: The Freedom of the Hills, Fifth Edition*. Seattle: The Mountaineers, 1992.

Houston, C. *High Altitude: Illness and Wellness*. Merrillville, IN: ICS Books, Inc., 1993.

Lentz, M.J., Macdonald, S.C., and Carline, J.D. *Mountaineering First Aid*. Seattle: The Mountaineers, 1990.

Merry, W. *The Wilderness First-Aid Guide*. Ontario: McClelland & Stewart, Inc.: 1994.

Nelson, S. and Nelson, R. *Easy Field Guide to Common Snakes of Arizona*. Phoenix: Primer Publishers, 1985.

Nelson, S. and Nelson, R. *Easy Field Guide to Common Desert Insects of Arizona*. Phoenix: Primer Publishers, 1992.

Notes, *Ninth Annual Wilderness Emergencies Conference*. Flagstaff, AZ: October 1994.

Schimelpfenig, T., and Lindsey, L. *NOLS Wilderness First Aid*. Harrisburg, PA: Stackpole, 1991.

Setnicka, T.J. *Wilderness Search and Rescue*. Boston: Appalachian Mountain Club, 1980.

Stewart, C.E. *Environmental Emergencies*. Baltimore: Williams and Wilkins, 1990.

Trefz, B.W. *The ABC's of CPR: Save a Life*. Park Ridge, IL: American Academy of Orthopaedic Surgeons, 1988.

Wilkerson, J.A. (Ed.). *Medicine for Mountaineering & Other Wilderness Activities: Fourth Edition*. Seattle: The Mountaineers, 1992.

INDEX

A

ABCD's 2-5
—airway 2
—breathing 4
—circulation 4
—disabilities 4
ASR. *See* Autonomic stress response
Abrasions 58
Acute mountain sickness 106-107
AEIOUTIPS 13
Airway 2-4
Altitude acclimatization 108
Altitude Illness 105-110
—acute mountain sickness 106-107
—high altitude cerebral edema (HACE) 107
—high altitude pulmonary edema (HAPE) 107-108
—physiology 105-106
—prevention 108-109
AMPLE 12-13
Amputation 60
Anaphylaxis 16, 18, 20, 78
Ankle sprains, treatment for 54-55
Arachnids 79-81
—scorpions 81
—spiders. *See* Spiders
Autonomic stress response 16-17
—parasympathetic 17
—sympathetic 17
AVPU 9
Avulsion 60

B

Battle's sign. *See* Head injuries

C

D

S

T

V

W